M000228289

RED

THE COLOR OF

Christmas

RED

THE COLOR OF
Christmas

GREG LAURIE

KERYGMA
PUBLISHING

ALLEN
DAVID
BOOKS

Copyright © 2012 by Greg Laurie. All rights reserved.

International Standard Book Number: 978-1-61291-352-0

Published by Kerygma Publishing

Cover design by RJS Design Studio
Coordination: FM Management, Ltd.
Contact: mgf@fmmgt.net

No part of this publication may be reproduced, stored in a retrieval system, or transmitted, in any form or by any means — electronic, mechanical, photocopying, recording, or otherwise — without prior written permission.

Unless otherwise indicated, all Scripture quotations are taken from the New King James Version (NKJV). Copyright © 1982 by Thomas Nelson, Inc. Used by permission. All rights reserved.

Scripture quotations marked (NLT) are taken from The New Living Translation, copyright © 1996, 2004, 2007 by Tyndale House Foundation. Used by permission of Tyndale House, Inc., Carol Stream, Illinois, 60188. All rights reserved.

Scripture quotations marked (NIV) are taken from the HOLY BIBLE, NEW INTERNATIONAL VERSION®. Copyright © 1973, 1978, 1984 by Biblica. Used by permission of Zondervan. All rights reserved.

Scripture quotations marked (TLB) are taken from The Living Bible, copyright © 1971 by Tyndale House Publishers, Wheaton, Illinois.

Scripture quotations marked (MSG) are taken from The Message. Copyright © 1993, 1994, 1995, 1996, 2000, 2001, 2002. Used by permission of NavPress Publishing Group. All rights reserved.

Scripture quotations marked (PH) are taken from J. B. Phillips, "The New Testament in Modern English," 1962 edition, published by HarperCollins.

Printed in China

1 2 3 4 5 6 7 / 17 16 15 14 13 12

CONTENTS

INTRODUCTION: The Color of Christmas   7

Part 1: Christmas BC

1. Before Bethlehem   13
2. What's in a Name?   37
3. Gabriel's Two Visits   55
4. A Twisted Family Tree   77

Part 2: Christmas Lost and Found

5. Don't Miss Christmas   105
6. Don't Lose Jesus   127
7. What the Wise Men Understood   145
8. What the Shepherds Found   161
9. The Promise of Christmas   173
10. Be Ready for His Coming   201

CONCLUSION: God with Us   219
NOTES   229

INTRODUCTION

THE COLOR OF CHRISTMAS

We have all wondered from time to time whether we might have missed the real meaning of Christmas.

People say, "It's too commercial." Or maybe, "It's too materialistic." Others of us say, "It's become too politically correct."

One thing we might not have considered is this: Perhaps we've made it too beautiful.

Most of us, whether we grew up in a Christian home or not, can call to mind Christmas card images of snowy countrysides, horse-drawn sleighs, wreaths of holly, frosty windows, red candles, rosy-cheeked carolers clad in scarves and hats, and softly glowing colored lights. Besides these, we have all the lovely biblical images as well: mother and Child, animals in the stable, adoring shepherds, and richly robed wise men following a wondrous star across the heavens.

It's all so beautiful.

And in many ways, the first Christmas *was* beautiful.

But here's what we might forget: The beautiful Baby born in the manger at Bethlehem came with a distinct purpose. That mission was to grow up and, in the very prime of His life, surrender Himself to the horrors of a Roman cross, shed His blood, and die for the sins of the world.

Yes, there is much wonder and beauty in what God accomplished on that Christmas two thousand-plus years ago, and we're right to be in awe of it. But all of heaven knew the real reason why Jesus came to earth and was born as a human baby. It wasn't just to teach everyone to be good and love his or her neighbor; it was to die an agonizing death to ransom us from an eternal death sentence.

He came as a Redeemer.

The shadow of the cross lay over the beauty of that first Christmas night.

Think of Mary, proudly carrying her newborn Son into the temple to have Him circumcised according to the Law. An old man named Simeon took the Child in his arms and prophesied over Him, speaking of light and salvation and glory. But before he turned away, he had a sober message for Mary: "Yes, a sword will pierce through your own soul also" (Luke 2:35).

Within the joy, within the wonder, there is also pain—and the red blood paid to redeem us.

At Christmas we decorate our trees with festive lights and ornaments. But the real "tree" in the Christmas story wasn't beautiful at all; it was a cruel instrument of execution, used to bring about the death of God's Son. The Bible says, "Cursed is everyone who hangs on a tree" (Galatians 3:13). Jesus hung on that tree and "became sin for us." He was born to die that we might live.

Isaiah 1:18 says, "'Come now, and let us reason together,' says the Lord, 'Though your sins are like scarlet, they shall be as white as snow; though they are red like crimson, they shall be as wool.'"

Red is the color of Christmas.

It's not because Santa wore red or because we wrap our presents in red paper or attach red bows on top of holly wreaths or put red bulbs and lights on our trees. Red is the color of Christmas for a different reason altogether, and it doesn't fit in with the way our culture celebrates December 25. The Christmas color of red isn't random; it is the color of the blood that flowed from the wounds of Jesus Christ as He died for the sins of the world, making available to you the greatest gift you could ever receive in a billion years.

The apostle Paul said, "Thank God for this gift, his gift. No language can praise it enough!"[1]

This is truly the only gift that literally keeps on giving, the gift of eternal life through Jesus Christ our Lord. Augustine put it best: "Son of God became son of man, so that you who were sons of men might be made sons of God."

Jesus was born, lived, died, and rose again from the dead so that you could come into a relationship with God, receive the gift of eternal life, and live a life of meaning and purpose.

That is the real message of Christmas. Let every glimpse of red remind you of the greatest Gift of all.

PART 1

* * * * * * * * * * * * * *

CHRISTMAS BC

1

BEFORE BETHLEHEM

I love the Christmas story and never get tired of hearing it or telling it. It is the most powerful of all stories. And best of all, it's completely true!

But the real story of Christmas goes way, way back before Bethlehem, before Mary and Joseph, before the shepherds and wise men and innkeeper and King Herod and all of the people who played a part at that great hinge of history two thousand years ago.

In fact, the first mention of Christmas was BC.

BC?

How could that be? Doesn't BC stand for "Before Christ"? How could there be a Christmas story before Jesus came?

The answer is simply this: The story of Christmas is actually an integral part of an even greater story that goes all the way back

13

to the beginning. It is the story of our redemption.

Interestingly enough, the account in Scripture begins with a tree — not a Christmas tree, but "the tree of the knowledge of good and evil." God Himself placed that tree in the midst of the Garden of Eden, the incredible paradise where our first parents, Adam and Eve, lived.

Those first two human beings experienced radiant beauty at every turn of those garden paths, with stunning trees, soft breezes, and magnificent flowers — most likely beyond what we have ever seen or even imagined. They also had exotic wildlife, the companionship of the animal kingdom, with creatures that would never and could never hurt them. Best of all by far, they enjoyed unbroken, daily fellowship with their Creator. The world at that time was completely free of sin and all the guilt, shame, grief, and dark shadows that accompany it.

And what was Adam and Eve's assignment? Basically, they were to discover, oversee, and enjoy all that God had placed in that lovely heaven-on-earth.

But there was one prohibition. Just one: "But the LORD God warned him, 'You may freely eat the fruit of every tree in the garden — except the tree of the knowledge of good and evil. If you eat its fruit, you are sure to die'" (Genesis 2:16-17, NLT).

Most of us have heard how Adam and Eve stood by that tree and listened to the voice of the tempter, who suggested they would do well to disobey God and eat of the fruit that He had restricted. He hissed, "You won't die! . . . God knows that your eyes will be opened as soon as you eat it, and you will be like God, knowing both good and evil" (Genesis 3:4-5, NLT).

The tragic record goes on to state,

> *The woman was convinced. She saw that the tree was beautiful and its fruit looked delicious, and she wanted the wisdom it would give her. So she took some of the fruit and ate it. Then she gave some to her husband, who was with her, and he ate it, too. At that moment their eyes were opened, and they suddenly felt shame at their nakedness. So they sewed fig leaves together to cover themselves. (verses 6-7, NLT)*

Their eyes were opened, all right. Satan was correct about that part. But they did not become "like God." In fact, they lost the most precious possession in their lives, far more important than their beautiful Eden or even each other. They lost that sweet fellowship with their Creator.

> *When the cool evening breezes were blowing, the man and his wife heard the LORD God walking about in the garden. So they hid from the LORD God among the trees. Then the LORD God called to the man, "Where are you?"*
>
> *He replied, "I heard you walking in the garden, so I hid. I was afraid because I was naked."*
>
> *"Who told you that you were naked?" the LORD God asked.*

"Have you eaten from the tree whose fruit I commanded you not to eat?" (verses 8-11, NLT)

What followed was the first miserable excuse in all of human history. And wouldn't you know it? It began with a man complaining about his wife and was followed with "the devil made me do it."

The man replied, "It was the woman you gave me who gave me the fruit, and I ate it."

Then the LORD God asked the woman, "What have you done?"

"The serpent deceived me," she replied. "That's why I ate it."

(verses 12-13, NLT)

What follows is the first Christmas verse in the Bible. No, it's not Isaiah 9:6, that well-loved passage that prophesies the coming of Jesus as Wonderful, Counselor, Mighty God, Everlasting Father, and Prince of Peace. Nor is it Micah 5:2, which speaks of little Bethlehem among the thousands of Judah.

The fact is, you may have never heard of Genesis 3:15 referred to as a Christmas passage, but that's just what it is. Why? Because it's the very first verse in the Bible that speaks of a Coming One who would accomplish our salvation.

It is the first *red* verse in Scripture.

The words come from God Himself and are directed at Satan:

I will put enmity
Between you and the woman,
And between your seed and her Seed;
He shall bruise your head,
And you shall bruise His heel.

By these words, God was drawing the battle lines and saying, "Game on." The Lord was telling the devil that a Coming One would crush his head. Yes, the evil one would bruise His heel, but in the process, the Redeemer would smash the head of Satan.

From that time forward, then, Satan has been watching and waiting for this expected Deliverer, the Christ, the Messiah. And knowing as he did that this Savior would come through the Jewish people, he did everything in his power to stop the birth of the Promised One before it could happen. You can trace it right through the Old Testament. In the book of Exodus you find Pharaoh, king of Egypt, systematically executing all the newborn baby boys. But ultimately, the Lord raised up Moses to go back to Egypt and lead His people out of that land in a great exodus.

Then you fast-forward to the book of Esther, and you see the plot of the wicked man known as Haman, who wanted to execute all of the Jews. It's so easy to see the hand of Satan in this.

Haman began with wanting revenge on one lone Jew, Mordecai, but he became swallowed up by rage that knew no bounds and tried to kill every Jew in the world.

Over in the New Testament, in the gospel of Matthew, we have the plot of King Herod to kill all the baby boys in the region of Bethlehem, two years old and under. He had received word from the traveling Magi about a coming King who would be born in that town. Inspired by Satan, he tried to kill the Messiah by slaughtering all the baby boys in the vicinity.

Bloody and horrific as these attempts may have been, no one and nothing could stop the Messiah from being born, because God always keeps His appointments. And at the right moment the Lord came to us, born in that manger in Bethlehem. As it says in the book of Galatians, "When the fullness of the time had come, God sent forth His Son, born of a woman" (4:4).

Yet was that where Jesus "began"?

Jesus in the "Before" Days

Did Jesus preexist before Bethlehem? Was there a Jesus before the Nativity?

The answer is yes.

Bethlehem is where the incarnation took place—when God became a man. But that is *not* when Jesus came into being. Jesus is God, and as God, He is eternal; He always has been and He always will be. In the book of Revelation, He says, "I am the First and the Last. I am the Living One; I was dead, and behold I am alive for ever and ever!" (1:17-18, NIV).

Even though both Matthew and Luke chose to begin their gospels with the birth of Christ, John's gospel begins by going back before, before, before, to the very beginning of everything:

> *In the beginning was the Word, and the Word was with God, and the Word was God. He was in the beginning with God. All things were made through Him, and without Him nothing was made that was made. In Him was life, and the life was the light of men. And the light shines in the darkness, and the darkness did not comprehend it.* (verses 1-5)

Most of our Bible translations have a definite article before the word *beginning*. We read, "In *the* beginning was the Word." In the original language, however, there is no definite article. That means you cannot pinpoint the moment in time when there was a beginning, because John is looking all the way back through time to eternity past. He is going back further than our minds can imagine.

Jesus existed before there was a world, before there were planets, stars, and galaxies, before there was light and darkness, before there was any matter whatsoever. The Godhead is eternal; Jesus Christ is coequal, coeternal, and coexistent with the Father and the Holy Spirit. He was with God. He was God. He *is* God.

When Jesus entered our world as a human being, He became an embryo, and then . . . deity in diapers. Jesus left the safety of heaven, stepped into time and space, breathed our air, shared our pain, walked in our shoes, lived our life, and died our death.

Jesus did not become identical to us, but He did identify with us. In fact, He could not have identified with us any more closely than He did. It was total identification without the loss of identity, for He became one of us without ceasing to be Himself. He became human without ceasing to be God.

It sort of blows the mind to think about, but Jesus Christ was fully God *and* fully man. Now when I say "fully man," I don't mean that He had the capacity to sin. Being God, that could not or would not happen. Yet He was a man in a human body, feeling human emotion, facing physical limitations, and experiencing real pain. Though actual blood coursed through His veins, He was and is deity — God in human form.

The old Christmas carol said it well:

Veiled in flesh, the Godhead see
Hail the incarnate Deity
Pleased as man with men to dwell
Jesus, our Emmanuel

John 1 tells us that "the Word was with God." This literally means that "the word was *continually toward* God." This gives us a glimpse into the relationship of Father, Son, and Holy Spirit. The preposition *with* carries the idea of nearness along with a sense of movement toward God. That's another way of saying there always has been the deepest equality and intimacy within the Trinity. Jesus summed it up in John 17 when He prayed to the Father, saying, "And now, O Father, glorify Me together with Yourself, with the glory which I had with You before the world was" (verse 5).

One popular paraphrase reads like this:

And now, Father, glorify me with your very own splendor,
The very splendor I had in your presence
Before there was a world. (MSG)

Before there was a world!

There never was a time when Christ did not exist. Yet this eternal Son of God became a man, and that is what we celebrate at Christmas. In Isaiah 9:6, written centuries before the Lord's birth in Bethlehem, the prophet says of Him, "For unto us a Child is born, unto us a Son is given." This passage perfectly sums up what happened on Christmas, giving us both the heavenly and the earthly perspective. We tend to view Christmas from our viewpoint: the Child being born. But then Isaiah gives it

from the heavenly perspective: a Son is given. Christmas, then, is
the story of an arrival, but it is also the story of a departure. He
arrived on earth, but He departed from heaven.

BC Appearances of Jesus

The theologians have a word for it: *theophany*. What it means is
an appearance of God.

We might also use the word *Christophany*, which means an
appearance of Christ before Bethlehem.

Are all theophanies Christophanies?

Maybe, because the apostle tells us that "no one has ever seen
God, but God the One and Only, who is at the Father's side, has
made him known" (John 1:18, NIV). When God makes an appearance in the Old Testament, we can assume that it's Jesus, the Son
of God.

How do we know He did this?

Consider this exchange that Jesus had with the Jewish leaders, who were all for holding onto Abraham but rejecting Jesus.
The Lord speaks first here:

*"Your father Abraham rejoiced at the thought of seeing my day; he
saw it and was glad."*

*"You are not yet fifty years old," the Jews said to him, "and
you have seen Abraham!"*

*"I tell you the truth," Jesus answered, "before Abraham was
born, I am!" (John 8:56-58, NIV)*

The Lord was indicating that at some point in His life, the
patriarch Abraham met Him in what we call a preincarnate
appearance.

For me, the account of the two disciples on the Emmaus road
in the gospel of Luke really settles the issue of Jesus' making
multiple appearances in the Old Testament. Do you remember
that remarkable story?

*Now that same day two of them were going to a village called
Emmaus, about seven miles from Jerusalem. They were talking with
each other about everything that had happened. As they talked and
discussed these things with each other, Jesus himself came up and
walked along with them; but they were kept from recognizing him.*

*He asked them, "What are you discussing together as you
walk along?"*

*They stood still, their faces downcast. One of them, named
Cleopas, asked him, "Are you only a visitor to Jerusalem and do
not know the things that have happened there in these days?"*

"What things?" he asked.

*"About Jesus of Nazareth," they replied. "He was a prophet,
powerful in word and deed before God and all the people. The chief
priests and our rulers handed him over to be sentenced to death, and*

they crucified him; but we had hoped that he was the one who was going to redeem Israel. And what is more, it is the third day since all this took place. In addition, some of our women amazed us. They went to the tomb early this morning but didn't find his body. They came and told us that they had seen a vision of angels, who said he was alive. Then some of our companions went to the tomb and found it just as the women had said, but him they did not see."

He said to them, "How foolish you are, and how slow of heart to believe all that the prophets have spoken! Did not the Christ have to suffer these things and then enter his glory?" And beginning with Moses and all the Prophets, he explained to them what was said in all the Scriptures concerning himself. (Luke 24:13-27, NIV)

Wow, wouldn't you have loved to listen in on *that* conversation? He took them through all the passages in the Bible that allude to Messiah: the types, the pictures, and no doubt the Christophanies themselves. I wish someone could have followed about two paces behind that little group, recording them on an iPhone. (And I wish that someone could have been me.) When I get to heaven, I definitely would love to have a conversation just like that one with Jesus.

Appearing to Abraham

Let's consider some potential Christophanies—appearances of Jesus before Bethlehem. The first is found in Genesis 22, the story of Abraham and Isaac on Mount Moriah. At the time of this incident, Abraham and Sarah were quite old, yet the Lord revealed to them that they were going to have a son in their old age.

When the boy was born, they named him Isaac, or "Laughter," because they were filled with joy beyond words. The little boy brought great happiness into their home, and he became the apple of his father's eye.

That is why it seemed almost unimaginable when the Lord came to him with a request that must have shaken the old man to his core:

> "Abraham!" God called.
>
> "Yes," he replied. "Here I am."
>
> "Take your son, your only son — yes, Isaac, whom you love so much — and go to the land of Moriah. Go and sacrifice him as a burnt offering on one of the mountains, which I will show you."
> (verses 1-2, NLT)

The Bible says that God was testing Abraham's faith. Had the old patriarch allowed young Isaac to become an idol in his life? Perhaps. It's possible for any of us to allow things or people to become more important to us than God Himself — even a wife or a husband, a son or a daughter.

All of this, of course, was an Old Testament picture of what would happen some two thousand years later at the cross of Calvary, where God would offer His own Son. This passage gives us two views of the same event. It gives us the perspective of Abraham, who was willing to obey God and do what He required. But we can also learn from Isaac's point of view. Isaac was a young man at this point and would have been able to resist his elderly dad if he had chosen to. So as they were on their journey and nearing the place of sacrifice on the mountain, he realized that they had no animal with them and may have wondered if he would be the one offered up on that altar.

Isaac could have said, "You know, Dad, I've been thinking about this. I think it makes more sense for *you* to be the sacrifice instead of me. After all, you're old and I'm young. You've seen your day, but I haven't had much of a chance at life. Why don't we flip this thing around, and I will sacrifice you?"

But Isaac didn't say anything like that. To his credit, he submitted himself to the will of his father, even to the point of being bound and lying on the altar. What trust! And as Abraham raised that knife and was about to bring it down on his own son, the Lord suddenly intervened. In Genesis 22:11-12 we read,

> At that moment the angel of the LORD called to him from heaven, "Abraham! Abraham!"
>
> "Yes," Abraham replied. "Here I am!"

"Don't lay a hand on the boy!" the angel said. "Do not hurt him in any way, for now I know that you truly fear God. You have not withheld from me even your son, your only son." (NLT)

I believe this was a Christophany. The text doesn't refer to just any angel, but to "the angel of the LORD." And notice that He speaks as God, saying, "You have not withheld from *me* even your son." I believe this was Jesus Himself, intervening at this strategic moment—which was a perfect picture of what He Himself would experience at the cross of Calvary. Abraham was prepared to offer his son, his beloved child of promise. And Jesus said in John 3:16, "For God so loved the world that He gave His only begotten Son, that whoever believes in Him should not perish but have everlasting life."

A Wrestling Match with Jacob

Over in Genesis 32, the Bible gives us what I believe is yet another Christophany in the account of Jacob's wrestling with a Visitor from heaven.

Jacob, the son of Isaac and the grandson of Abraham, found himself alone one momentous night, camping out by the stream called Jabbok. You can read the full story in Scripture, but on this particular night, Jacob was more afraid than he had ever been in his life. He had endured some difficult and bitter years. Now in midlife, he felt like the weight of the world was resting on his shoulders; he feared for his family, he feared the uncertain future that lay ahead of him, and he feared for his very life.

That's where we pick up the story:

> *So Jacob was left alone, and a man wrestled with him till daybreak. When the man saw that he could not overpower him, he touched the socket of Jacob's hip so that his hip was wrenched as he wrestled with the man. Then the man said, "Let me go, for it is daybreak."*
>
> *But Jacob replied, "I will not let you go unless you bless me."*
>
> *The man asked him, "What is your name?"*
>
> *"Jacob," he answered.*
>
> *Then the man said, "Your name will no longer be Jacob, but Israel, because you have struggled with God and with men and have overcome."*
>
> *Jacob said, "Please tell me your name."*
>
> *But he replied, "Why do you ask my name?" Then he blessed him there.*
>
> *So Jacob called the place Peniel, saying, "It is because I saw God face to face, and yet my life was spared." (verses 24-30, NIV)*

I don't think Jacob was wrestling with an angel here; I think Jacob was wrestling with Jesus.

That night began for Jacob in solitude and an intense prayer time (see verses 9-12). And then he had an up-close-and-personal encounter with Jesus Christ that would change his life. It's often that way for us, isn't it? Our life circumstances force us into a corner—and perhaps a very frightening, intimidating corner. Do we cry out to God in that moment, or do we try to battle it through on our own, relying on our own strength and wisdom?

That's a very, very important question; in fact, your life may hinge on how you respond in that moment of great fear and pressure. Jacob turned to the Lord, the God of his father and grandfather. He meant business with God, and God meant business with him.

Obviously, the Lord was never in any danger of being pinned in that wrestling match with Jacob. (It would have been like Hulk Hogan wrestling with a five-year-old.) In the struggle, however, Jacob's hip was wrenched, making him disabled. By the end of the night, he was clinging to the Lord, crying out, "I will not let You go unless You bless me." Jacob had gone from fighting to submitting, from resisting to resting, and that was what God had been waiting for. Jacob had spent much of his life fighting with God, but he finally surrendered. As a result, the Lord gave him a new name.

I want you to note in verse 28 that the Lord said to Jacob, "You have struggled with God."

Jacob acknowledged that and said that he had seen God (see verse 30). I think this is a clear reference to a Christophany, a before-Bethlehem appearance of our Lord Jesus Christ.

Are you wrestling with God? Sometimes in our humanity and in our foolishness, that is what we do. God clearly reveals His will to us, and we say, "But I don't want that. I want *my* will. I want to do it *my* way." And we find ourselves wrestling with God throughout years of our lives. How much better it is when we surrender to His will.

It was Corrie ten Boom who said, "Don't wrestle. Just nestle." Don't fight with the One who has your best interests in mind.

A Message for Mr. and Mrs. Manoah

Samson's life began with a miracle. The parents of that famous strong man and judge of Israel had been unable to have children, which was a source of great shame and grief to people in that era.

Then one day, on what probably was a very ordinary day in every other respect, Mrs. Manoah had an amazing visitor:

> The angel of the LORD appeared to Manoah's wife and said, "Even though you have been unable to have children, you will soon become pregnant and give birth to a son. So be careful; you must not drink wine or any other alcoholic drink nor eat any forbidden food. You will become pregnant and give birth to a son, and his hair must never be cut. For he will be dedicated to God as a Nazirite from birth. He will begin to rescue Israel from the Philistines."
>
> The woman ran and told her husband, "A man of God appeared to me! He looked like one of God's angels, terrifying to see. I didn't ask where he was from, and he didn't tell me his name." (Judges 13:3-6, NLT)

Mrs. Manoah wasn't sure of whom she had just seen.

I believe she was seeing Jesus.

Manoah, who hadn't yet seen this mysterious heavenly Visitor, prayed that God would send Him again, and He did. Manoah asked for the Visitor's name and received this reply: "Why do you ask My name, seeing it is wonderful?" (verse 18).

After this, Manoah and his wife brought an offering of thanksgiving to the Lord. And as the flame was going up, the Lord ascended into the flame and went up to heaven. Manoah was immediately seized with panic, crying out, "We shall surely die, because we have seen God!" (verse 22).

Manoah and his wife knew they had seen more than a man of God and more than an angel. They knew in their hearts they had seen the living God Himself. And when they asked the Visitor His name, He replied that it was "wonderful." Where have we heard that before? In Isaiah 9:6, which prophesies the coming of the Messiah, we read, "His name will be called Wonderful, Counselor, Mighty God."

By the way, the word *wonderful,* given to Manoah that day, is the very same Hebrew word used in Isaiah 9:6 and means "surpassing or beyond human ability to understand."

I find it interesting how the Lord withheld His name from Manoah and did not reveal who He was. In the Old Testament, Christ is concealed, but in the New Testament, Christ is revealed.

In C. S. Lewis's classic book *The Voyage of the Dawn Treader*, there is a powerful scene near the end of the story when Aslan the great lion (who represents Christ) tells Lucy and Edmund they are too old to come back to Narnia and must live out their lives in England.

Through her tears, Lucy says, "It isn't Narnia, you know. It's you. We shan't meet you there. And how can we live, never meeting you?"

Aslan replies that they will meet him again, and that he is in their world, too.

Then he says, "But there I have another name. . . . This was the very reason why you were brought to Narnia, that by knowing me here for a little, you may know me better there."[1]

In other words, their eyes would be opened, and they would come to know Jesus Himself. In the story of Manoah, the Lord's identity was concealed. But it has now been revealed in what would become known as the New Covenant.

His Presence in the Flames

In my opinion, there is another dramatic Christophany in the story of Shadrach, Meshach, and Abed-Nego, three Jewish teenagers who followed the Lord. After the little nation of Judah was conquered by mighty Babylon, many of the Jews were taken into captivity in that enemy city and remained there for seventy years. Nebuchadnezzar, the king of Babylon, singled out the three young men to enter into his service, grooming them to become leaders in the kingdom someday.

He enrolled them in Babylonian University, desiring to school them in all the ways of that twisted, godless culture. Nebuchadnezzar had a massive golden image of himself erected, and at the dedication he commanded everyone in his kingdom to bow down before it and worship—or be put to death. In terror of their lives, all the people obediently fell before this image, except for Shadrach, Meshach, and Abed-Nego.

Refusing to bow, these three young Hebrews stood out like sore thumbs, and their shocking refusal was immediately reported to the king. Outraged, Nebuchadnezzar had them hauled into his royal presence and told them they had better bow down or he would have them thrown into a fiery furnace.

They were polite and respectful, but all three of them made it very clear they never would bow before an image of gold.

Let's pick up the story in Scripture:

And these three men, Shadrach, Meshach, and Abed-Nego, fell down bound into the midst of the burning fiery furnace.

Then King Nebuchadnezzar was astonished; and he rose in haste and spoke, saying to his counselors, "Did we not cast three men bound into the midst of the fire?"

They answered and said to the king, "True, O king."

"Look!" he answered, "I see four men loose, walking in the

midst of the fire; and they are not hurt, and the form of the fourth is
like the Son of God." (Daniel 3:23-25)

I believe that was a Christophany—that Jesus Himself was
walking with His boys through the fire.

And do you know what? He still does that. Jesus will walk
with you through your fire, whatever that fire may be. In
Isaiah 43:2-3, we read these words:

When you pass through the waters, I will be with you;
And through the rivers, they shall not overflow you.
When you walk through the fire, you shall not be burned,
Nor shall the flame scorch you.
For I am the LORD your God,
The Holy One of Israel, your Savior.

We are never alone in life.

This is the message we see from Genesis to Revelation. Jesus
Christ has always been there. He came to Abraham at the
moment of supreme crisis. He came to Jacob when the weight of
the world was on his shoulders. He came to Samson's parents,
who had imagined their situation to be hopeless. He came to
the three Hebrew young men in the midst of the flames, and
they walked through that fire without even getting their robes
singed.

Then, in the fullness of time, He came to earth as a human being: a little Baby, placed in a manger of hay. He grew up, clear-eyed and strong, knowing that all along, there was a cross in His future and He would lay down His life for your sins and my sins.

Rising from the dead, He is now with us always. In Hebrews 13:5, He says, "I will never leave you nor forsake you." And in Matthew 28:20, He says, "Surely I am with you always, to the very end of the age" (NIV).

WHAT'S IN A NAME?

I heard a story about a guy who got stuck with the last name of Odd.

Can you imagine going through life with a name like that?

"So . . . your last name is Odd. That's odd."

"Hey, you're kind of *Odd*, aren't you?"

He just hated it. So after living with that miserable name his whole life, he actually gave instructions that upon his death, nothing be written on his tombstone. "Just leave it blank," he had instructed, because he couldn't bear the thought of people walking through the cemetery, seeing his last name, and continuing to say, "That's odd."

So sure enough, honoring his wishes, they gave him a blank tombstone. A blank tombstone, however, is an unusual thing, and people walking through the cemetery would notice that featureless piece of granite.

And they would say, "That's odd."

What's in name? It all depends on what your name is. If you have gone through life with a name that you didn't appreciate, you know that names can really make a difference. In the Old Testament, a man with the name of Jabez (which means "Pain") made lemonade out of sour lemons. He used his name as a springboard to cry out to God for a special blessing, and the Lord answered his request (see 1 Chronicles 4:9-10).

Most people, however, don't have the determination or faith of Jabez. One psychiatrist studied the names of 15,000 juvenile delinquents and discovered that those with odd or embarrassing names were in trouble four times as much as the others.

I had to go through life with the last name of Laurie—which is a girl's name, right? I would always—I mean, every time—be asked to spell it.

"What's your name?"

"Greg Laurie."

"Laurie?"

"Laurie."

"How do you spell it?"

"L-a-u-r-i-e."

"That's a girl's name."

"Yes, it is."

So maybe you, like me, went through life with a name you

didn't like. Or maybe you got stuck with a nickname. I had the weirdest nickname of all: *Pogo.* So I was Pogo Laurie. (Don't you dare call me that, by the way. I will not answer to that.)

With the passing of time, certain names become popular. A couple of generations ago, names like Bob and Charles were popular. During the 1960s, many people rebelled against traditional names. I heard about a survey taken among those who lived in hippie communes. Here are some of the names they actually gave to their poor kids: Carrot, Sunshine, Fender, Gravy, and Doobie.

Can you imagine naming your kid Doobie?

The current trend is to find the coolest name — something of a designer name — for a baby. Or perhaps a name that no one has ever used before. Apparently, some of the more cautious parents are doing Internet searches on the names they are thinking of giving to their kids. One parent said, "Nobody wants their baby's name to turn out to be a serial killer in Nebraska."

The top names for girls right now include Abigail, Emily, Madison, Chloe, Ava, Olivia, Isabella, and Sophia. The most popular names for boys are Logan, Lucas, Noah, Ethan, Jaden, Jacob, Liam, Mason, Jackson, and Aiden.

Then there are those weird parents who have interesting last names and think it will be clever to give their child a funny first name to match (I'm not making these up): Chris B. Bacon, Eileen Dover, Gene Pool, Douglas Fir, Alba Tross, Anita Hug, Bea Clown, and Cookie Cutter.

In biblical days, however, names really meant something.

Sometimes the name related to some physical attribute of the child at birth. For instance, in the book of Genesis, we know that Isaac and Rebecca's firstborn was named Esau, which means "hairy." And why was he named "Hairy"? Because that is how he looked when he came out of the womb! His twin brother came out after him, hanging on to Esau's heel. So they named this second boy Jacob, which means "heel catcher."

In the book of 1 Samuel, the wife of one of the priests gave birth to a baby in great stress after the news came that the Philistines had stolen the Ark of the Covenant. She named her baby "Ichabod," meaning "the glory has departed."

Can you imagine bringing a friend with that name home from school and introducing him to your mom? "Hey, Mom, this is my new friend, The-Glory-Has-Departed."

But now we come to the most important name of all: the name that was given to our Lord when the angel Gabriel came to Mary and told her that she was going to bring forth a Son.

The Name Above All Names

Do not be afraid, Mary, for you have found favor with God. And behold, you will conceive in your womb and bring forth a Son, and shall call His name JESUS. He will be great, and will be called the

Son of the Highest; and the Lord God will give Him the throne of
His father David. And He will reign over the house of Jacob for-
ever, and of His kingdom there will be no end. (Luke 1:30-33)

Jesus Christ is the name above all names. It is a name of great power. If you don't believe me, just say it sometime. Out loud. Say it in a crowded or noisy room. People might be all around you, talking like crazy. But when you say "Jesus Christ" or "In the name of Jesus Christ," you will be heard all over the room. People will turn to look. Conversations will stop.

The strange thing is, you could say "Buddha" or "Hare Krishna" or even "Joseph Smith" and not create a ripple. But say the name of Jesus, and something happens in that room.

The Bible says that one day, at the name of Jesus Christ, every knee will bow and every tongue will confess that He is the Lord, to the glory of God the Father (see Philippians 2:10-11).

In Isaiah 9, one of the great Christmas passages, we read a prophecy of the Lord's birth, and of the names or titles He will be given:

For unto us a Child is born,
Unto us a Son is given;
And the government will be upon His shoulder.
And His name will be called
Wonderful, Counselor, Mighty God,

Everlasting Father, Prince of Peace.
Of the increase of His government and peace
There will be no end,
Upon the throne of David and over His kingdom. (verses 6-7)

As we noted in the last chapter, Jesus Christ existed long before Bethlehem. As part of the Trinity, He has always existed and has no beginning or end. So the birth of our Lord was not when He began His existence. It was merely His entrance to planet Earth.

Each of the names or titles for Jesus recorded in the book of Isaiah not only gives us insight into who He is, but also into the purpose of God for each one of us. Think of these names like five gifts under your tree that God has for you.

His Name Is Wonderful

This takes care of the dullness of life.

The word *wonderful* comes from the root word *wonder*.

Bertrand Russell once claimed that at least half of the sins of mankind were caused by a fear of boredom.

Probably the number one thing that will be under most of our Christmas trees this year is something electronic—an iPhone, an iPad, a Kindle, or maybe a new digital camera. By the time this book is printed, there probably will be some new gadget on the market that didn't even exist when I began to write it. We never have had such advanced technology. Everywhere you go now, you see people with their eyes glued to their smartphones or tablets, checking out Facebook, reading e-mail, following Twitter, texting, or playing one of those addictive little games. And all the while, you will hear people saying, "I am really bored."

The wonder quickly drains away from even the latest, most cutting-edge electronic devices. In fact, they will be outdated almost from the moment they leave the shelf. Just after you buy your device, you will hear chatter about a newer version with more megapixels or battery life or apps or whatever.

In fact, the gifts that we have under the tree are a metaphor for life itself—in effect, there is nothing this world has to offer that will fill a void in our lives. No matter what you have, no matter what you are able to buy, it will never satisfy you. (Or at least, not for very long.) An article in *Wired* magazine said, "Our culture is about distraction, numbing oneself; there is no self-reflection, no sitting still. It's absolutely exhausting."[1]

We need God in our lives! He is the only One who will satisfy the emptiness and the deep-down longing for "something" we can't even put words to. Scripture reminds us to "be still and know that [He is] God" (Psalm 46:10). *The Message* renders that verse, "Step out of the traffic! Take a long, loving look at me, your High God." Despite all of the passing things of this world that will not last, there is Jesus, and He is *wonderful*.

His very name is Wonder.

At Christmas when we open our gifts, sometimes, frankly, we're a little disappointed. We wanted or expected one thing, only to receive something we didn't want or don't really care about. Or maybe we are disappointed by the reactions of those to whom we've given gifts. We hoped our gifts would be hits, but oftentimes they are misses, and we see that look of disappointment on their faces.

Life is full of letdowns, isn't it?

But God is never a letdown; God is wonderful.

We could pick that word *wonder* apart and see elements of surprise, astonishment, admiration, bewilderment, worship, and awe. We used to say that "God is awesome," but that word has lost some of its strength through overuse. What we really mean is that He inspires awe deep within us.

Our awesome God takes care of the dullness of our lives.

Medical science seeks to add years to your life, but only Jesus Christ can add life to your years and give you a life that is worth living. His name is wonderful.

His Name Is Counselor

This takes care of the decisions of life.

Did you know that God Almighty wants to personally give you direction? That He has a custom-designed plan just for you?

Think of all the places where people look for answers today. Some go to the local bar and pour out their troubles to anyone who will listen. Some go to psychics for direction or consult a horoscope. Others will fork out the money to go psychiatrists, psychologists, or life coaches.

I have read that during this time of the year, depression rates go up dramatically. More people check into hospitals. Suicide rates go up during the holiday season. One fifty-four-year-old woman who was seeking psychotherapy during the holidays made this statement: "I get sad at Christmas. I feel like there's a big gap in what it's supposed to be about spiritually. I don't feel that I want to get into this material glut. I think deep down inside, we are all afraid of dying. The terrorist attacks brought that home to us on a very large, horrendous scale."

Still others will even go to Google trying to find answers, typing in "What is the meaning of life?"

Help me, Google. Isn't that pitiful?

The iPhone 4S has a feature called Siri, which acts like a personal assistant, reminding you of appointments or directing you toward the closest coffee shop. Of course, I have one because I'm into gadgets and love all the newest bells and whistles.

So the other day I asked Siri, "What is the meaning of life?"

Siri (who has a woman's voice) answered, "I don't know, but I think there is an app for that." I asked her again, and she replied, "All evidence to date suggests it is chocolate."

So I said, "Siri, why am I here?"

And my electronic assistant answered, "I don't know, and frankly I have been wondering that myself."

Listen. You don't need to go to Google or Siri or a psychic or a psychologist for the answers of life. Everything you need to know about life and about God is found in the pages of your Bible; God will speak to you through His Word.

The Bible says of itself,

All Scripture is inspired by God and is useful to teach us what is true and to make us realize what is wrong in our lives. It corrects us when we are wrong and teaches us to do what is right. God uses it to prepare and equip his people to do every good work. (2 Timothy 3:16-17, NLT)

In Psalm 73, Asaph writes, "You guide me with your counsel, and afterward you will take me into glory" (verse 24, NIV). So in this life and in the next, you will find no better Counselor than your own Creator and Savior.

His Name Is Mighty God

This takes care of the demands of life.

Power is a big deal for men. Guys can never have too much power. If two men go to a gym, it's all about who can bench press the most or do the most curls.

Or if it's a car, it's about how much horsepower you have.
I have a friend who has a Shelby Mustang with 500 horsepower.
He let me drive it once in a big, empty parking lot, and I admit,
I coveted the car. With my friend riding shotgun, I put that baby
into first gear, floored it, and we almost went airborne. Then
I slammed it into second and threw it into third, and each time it
felt like we left the ground. It was great fun!

Afterward, he told me he was having more horsepower added
to it. When I asked him why in the world he would do that, he
smiled and said, "Bragging rights."

This sort of talk is even true among computer geeks. They're
saying to each other, "How much RAM do you have in that
thing? How much storage? How big is your hard drive?" It's
always about power.

When you think about it, the history of mankind has been
the story of acquiring, using, and abusing power. First it was
manpower. Then it was horse power, steam power, diesel power,
and nuclear power. What we seem to lack is *willpower*.

The Mighty God, however, is present with us to give us all
the power we need to live the Christian life.

Jesus wasn't a man who became God; that would be impossible. He was and is God who became a man. The all-powerful,
eternal Creator became a baby, as difficult as it may be to wrap
our minds around that thought.

Max Lucado summed it up this way:

Divinity arrived. Heaven opened herself and placed her most precious one in a human womb.

The omnipotent, in one instant, made Himself breakable. . . . He who was larger than the universe became an embryo. And He who sustains the world with a word chose to be dependent upon the nourishment of a young girl. . . . God had come near.[2]

That is what Christmas is all about. It's about the astounding, incomparable moment in human history when God became a man. Jesus was and is the mighty God, which takes care of all the demands of life. All the power that you will ever need to live the Christian life is available for you. As the apostle Peter wrote, "By his divine power, God has given us everything we need for living a godly life. We have received all of this by coming to know him, the one who called us to himself by means of his marvelous glory and excellence" (2 Peter 1:3, NLT).

Some people imagine that it must be really hard to be a Christian. I disagree with that assessment. Actually, it is *impossible* to be a Christian. It is absolutely beyond any of us apart from the help of the Holy Spirit. With His help, however, you can be the man or woman He has called you to be. As Jesus said, "With God all things are possible" (Matthew 19:26).

There will be many people opening electronic gizmos this Christmas, only to find that their new toys don't work. So they will look up the number for tech support and talk to someone on the phone (probably in India or Bangladesh). And those technicians are trained to always ask two questions before anything else. Question number one: Is the device plugged in? Question number two: Is the device turned on? You would be amazed at how many people's devices "don't work" because they are not plugged in or turned on.

God might ask the same of us. Are you plugged in? God will give you the power to live the life He has called you to live.

His Name Is Everlasting Father

This takes care of the future of life.

We know that life is more than what we are currently experiencing on this earth. In fact, the Bible teaches that you and I will live forever. That is a good thing, right?

Not necessarily.

It all depends on *where* you will live forever. You are an eternal soul. You are not a body that happens to have a soul; you are, as C. S. Lewis put it, a soul wrapped in a body. And the Bible teaches that one day your life on earth will end. If you are a believer in Jesus Christ, then your soul and your resurrected body will go into God's presence in heaven, where you will live with Him forever. But if you are not a believer, the Bible teaches that you will spend all eternity separated from God in a place called hell.

If you know the Everlasting Father, however, you don't have to be afraid of that.

Do you know Him in this way? Maybe you never got a chance to know your earthly father, which perhaps makes Christmas a difficult season for you. Maybe your dad walked out on the family, and you haven't seen him for years. Perhaps you were estranged from him at some point, and you have a very strange and strained relationship with him right now. When you think of God as being the Father, it's difficult to relate to that.

I can understand. I never knew my father growing up, never even knew who he was. I was conceived out of wedlock, and then my mom married and divorced seven different guys. Only one of them ever treated me as a father would treat a son. He was the one who adopted me and gave me my name Laurie. So I had a love for that man and was able to go back later in life, locate him, and lead him to Christ.

When I came to Jesus Christ, it was so great to realize there was a Father in heaven who always would be there for me, never abandon me, never desert me, and always take time for me.

When my father who adopted me died, God was there. When my mother died, God was there. When my son died, God was there. He always will be there for me, and He always will be there for you, because He is your Everlasting Father.

His Name Is Prince of Peace

This takes care of the disturbances of life.

In the storms of life, we long for peace. Life is filled with friction, hardship, and difficulty. There are troubled homes, troubled cities, and troubled people everywhere. But Jesus will be the Prince of Peace in your life. You won't find peace on a psychiatrist's couch, in a bottle, in a drug, in a human relationship, or in material possessions. You will find peace only in a relationship with God through Jesus Christ.

We remember the message the angels gave to the shepherds who were keeping watch over their flocks at night: "Glory to God in the highest, and on earth peace, goodwill toward men!" (Luke 2:14).

Yet when we look around at all the turmoil, strife, and anguish in our world, we might find ourselves asking, "Where is it? Where is that peace?" Even the town of Bethlehem is a very unsafe city at night. Where is the peace that the angels promised? Was it a joke? Were they mocking us?

No.

That statement of the angels could be better translated "Glory to God in the highest, and peace on earth *among men with whom God is well-pleased.*"

You see, all of the problems we witness and experience in the world today are the result of people and their disobedience to God. Humanity itself has brought about the violence, unrest, turmoil, and war on the planet. But despite those things, you and I can have peace in the midst of the most troubled times and difficult situations.

Even when chaos rages all around, even in the middle of the storm, you can have peace because the Lord *is* your peace. In John 14, Jesus said, "I am leaving you with a gift — peace of mind and heart. And the peace I give is a gift the world cannot give. So don't be troubled or afraid" (verse 27, NLT).

Do you have this peace that Jesus spoke of? The Bible describes it as the peace that passes all human understanding. But before you can have the peace *of* God you must first have peace *with* God, through Jesus Christ.

The Government Will Be on His Shoulder

Isaiah 9:6 tells us, "And the government will be upon His shoulder."

Yes, it *will* be. But it isn't yet.

There is a space of many years between "unto us a Child is born" and "the government will be upon His shoulder." We're still waiting for that latter statement to come to pass, because we know the government is *not* on His shoulder yet. Trust me on that! When He is in charge of the government, it will run incomparably better than it runs now.

The day is coming, however, when He will rule and reign on

this earth in righteousness. There will be no scandals. There will be no economic meltdowns. There will be no grandstanding for the media or political shenanigans. But that day is still coming; it is still future.

Before Jesus takes the government on His shoulders, He had to first take up the cross. And that's just what He did: He took that cross and died on it.

We like to think of the sweet little Baby in the manger and the singing angels and the visiting wise men, and all of those things are true. But if we miss *why* He came, we miss everything.

Before there was a planet called Earth, much less a garden called Eden or a city called Bethlehem, a decision was made in heaven. And the decision was that Jesus would come to this earth and die for us.

So what's in a name? It all depends on whose name it is. If it is the name of Jesus Christ, everything you need is in that name. The Bible says, "Whoever calls on the name of the Lord shall be saved" (Acts 2:21).

His name is Wonderful.

GABRIEL'S TWO VISITS

Gabriel Calls on Zechariah

It was a day like any other day when the supernatural invaded the natural.

Zechariah, the priest, was in the temple in Jerusalem, performing his priestly duties. The gospel of Luke tells us, "His order was on duty that week. As was the custom of the priests, he was chosen by lot to enter the sanctuary of the Lord and burn incense. While the incense was being burned, a great crowd stood outside, praying" (Luke 1:8-10, NLT).

So here was this elderly man, bringing the offering on behalf of the people of Israel. There were many priests in the nation at that time, so he would have considered it a high honor and real privilege to serve the Lord and the people in this way. He probably looked forward to going home that night and telling his wife, Elizabeth, all about it and what it had felt like to be in that holy place, representing the people before the God of Israel.

As it turned out, he had more to tell Elizabeth than he would have ever dreamed. The only trouble was, after that day, he wouldn't be able to speak!

As he was ministering in the temple, an angel of the Lord suddenly appeared to him, standing at the right side of the altar of incense. Understandably, the elderly priest was startled and probably froze in position with fear.

That's when the angel began to speak:

Don't be afraid, Zechariah! God has heard your prayer. Your wife, Elizabeth, will give you a son, and you are to name him John. You will have great joy and gladness, and many will rejoice at his birth, for he will be great in the eyes of the Lord. He must never touch wine or other alcoholic drinks. He will be filled with the Holy Spirit, even before his birth. And he will turn many Israelites to the Lord their God. He will be a man with the spirit and power of Elijah. He will prepare the people for the coming of the Lord. He will turn the hearts of the fathers to their children, and he will cause those who are rebellious to accept the wisdom of the godly.
(Luke 1:13-17, NLT)

The angel said, "God has heard your prayer." The way this verse reads in the original language seems to imply that God heard the prayer that Zechariah was praying *at that very moment.*

Had he been praying about having a son? Had he been expressing the secret longing of his heart to the Lord? Had he prayed that God might take away Elizabeth's disgrace among other women and allow her to bear a child?

It's possible, but then, why was he so doubtful when it was revealed to him that he and Elizabeth were going to have a son?

Then again, Zechariah may have been praying for the Messiah to arrive and finally deliver Israel. Many of his godly countrymen longed for the Promised One to come and deliver them from the iron heel of Rome. Perhaps Zechariah was praying in his heart, saying, *Lord, hear the prayers of Your people gathered outside this temple. They long for a Messiah. They long for a Deliverer and a Savior. Won't You please send Him to us?*

Suddenly Gabriel appeared, with news about that Messiah . . . and with an exciting personal word for Zechariah and his wife. Again, Gabriel had said, "God has heard your prayer."

To those of us who have walked with the Lord for years, it is not a surprise to hear that God answers prayer; we've seen countless answers to the requests and concerns we bring before Him. But sometimes it does surprise us when God answers our prayers *right away.*

Have you ever prayed for something and found yourself shocked that God actually answered it . . . almost immediately?

We've all experienced times when God doesn't say yes or no to our request, but something more like "Wait." He is saying, in effect, "That is a good request, but you aren't ready for that right now." Then there are other times when God will hear our prayer and say, "No, My child, I love you too much to give you what you just asked for."

Then there are times when the prayer is hardly out of our mouth and the answer comes right away. Bam! It's there! The phone rings or there's a knock on the door or a letter arrives or an e-mail pops up, and we receive the very thing we were just praying about.

If the truth were known, you and I often pray with a measure of doubt in our hearts. There is a good illustration of this in Acts 12, where James and Peter had both been arrested by King Herod and James had been put to death. I don't know if the church had been praying as fervently at that point as they should have been, but when they heard that James was gone, I'm sure they prayed very fervently for Peter, that God somehow would deliver him.

Did they realize that God was actually listening?

In a direct answer to their prayers, He dispatched an angel, who went to Peter's prison cell in the night. A heavenly light shone in that dark dungeon, and the iron shackles fell off Peter's wrists and legs. The door opened of its own accord, just like it does at Wal-Mart, and Peter walked out of prison, right past the sleeping guards and sentries.

Once out of jail, Peter hurried over to the house of John Mark, where he knew there would be a prayer meeting going on. And sure enough, there was. Looking this way and that to make sure he wasn't being followed, Peter knocked on the door. A servant girl named Rhoda answered.

She opened the door, and there stood Peter!

Instead of inviting him in, however, she closed the door in his face and ran into the back room, where men and women were praying for Peter with all their might.

Oh, Lord, be merciful to Peter.

Lord, please deliver our brother Peter.

God, Peter needs You right now. We pray for a miracle.

And at that very moment, the miracle they were praying for was still knocking on the door, trying to get in. When Rhoda gave the news, they told her she was crazy. How could Peter be at the door when Peter was in prison? Silly girl. It wasn't possible. Rhoda was seeing things.

But Rhoda kept insisting, "Guys, I'm telling you right now that Peter is standing at the front door!" Scripture tells us (and I love this) that they *all* went to the front door — the whole group!

The Bible says that when they saw Peter, "they were astonished" (verse 16).

If I were Peter, I think I would be just a little bit sarcastic, saying, "Hello, everybody! Are you going to leave me out here all night?"

These were good people who prayed fervently, but they must have prayed with some doubt too. When God answered their prayer so quickly, they were amazed.

I don't know what you may be facing right now as another Christmas rolls around. I don't know what burdens you might be carrying on your shoulders or what sort of trials you might be enduring. You need to bring those things continually before the Lord in prayer. The Bible tells us,

> Don't worry about anything; instead, pray about everything. Tell God what you need, and thank him for all he has done. Then you will experience God's peace, which exceeds anything we can understand. His peace will guard your hearts and minds as you live in Christ Jesus. (Philippians 4:6-7, NLT)

Zechariah had been praying, and as he was praying, God heard him, dispatching the mighty angel Gabriel with the answer.

It's just a little bit amazing to me that Zechariah had an angelic visitation, awesome as that must have been, and *still* expressed doubt about God answering his prayer.

Zechariah said to the angel, "How can I be sure this will happen? I'm an old man now, and my wife is also well along in years."

Then the angel said, "I am Gabriel! I stand in the very presence of God. It was he who sent me to bring you this good news! But now, since you didn't believe what I said, you will be silent and unable to speak until the child is born. For my words will certainly be fulfilled at the proper time." (Luke 1:18-20, NLT)

Zechariah was saying, "Well, hmmm, let's see. Have you considered the fact that I'm pretty old for something like that to happen? Does God realize that my wife is no spring chicken, either?"

I could find myself becoming pretty critical of Zechariah until I remember all the mighty things God has shown me through the years of my life, all the incredible answers to prayer I have seen, and yet I still struggle with doubt sometimes.

In the meantime, people outside the temple sanctuary were getting a little restless, wondering why the old fellow was taking so long. Had he died in there? What in the world was going on?

Suddenly Zechariah emerged, and he couldn't speak! The Bible says, "Then they realized from his gestures and his silence that he must have seen a vision in the sanctuary" (Luke 1:22, NLT). Did you ever wonder what kind of gestures Zechariah made to explain what he had seen? Did he flap his arms up and down to indicate an angel?

Whatever happened outside the sanctuary, Zechariah knew very well what had happened inside the sanctuary. First of all, wonder of wonders, he was going to be a daddy after all. (They would have to make his den into a nursery!) Even more significant than that, his little boy would grow up to be the forerunner of the Messiah, which meant the long-awaited Deliverer of Israel couldn't be far behind!

It was game on. The story was beginning to unfold.

Messiah was on His way.

Gabriel Visits Mary

Mary is the most privileged woman who ever lived, but she didn't live a privileged life. In fact, she lived in what you might call a "nothing town" in the middle of nowhere.

Now in the sixth month the angel Gabriel was sent by God to a city of Galilee named Nazareth, to a virgin betrothed to a man whose name was Joseph, of the house of David. The virgin's name was Mary. And having come in, the angel said to her, "Rejoice, highly favored one, the Lord is with you; blessed are you among women!"

But when she saw him, she was troubled at his saying, and considered what manner of greeting this was. Then the angel said to her, "Do not be afraid, Mary, for you have found favor with God. And behold, you will conceive in your womb and bring forth a

Son, and shall call His name JESUS. He will be great, and will be called the Son of the Highest; and the Lord God will give Him the throne of His father David. And He will reign over the house of Jacob forever, and of His kingdom there will be no end."

Then Mary said to the angel, "How can this be, since I do not know a man?"

And the angel answered and said to her, "The Holy Spirit will come upon you, and the power of the Highest will overshadow you; therefore, also, that Holy One who is to be born will be called the Son of God. Now indeed, Elizabeth your relative has also conceived a son in her old age; and this is now the sixth month for her who was called barren. For with God nothing will be impossible."

Then Mary said, "Behold the maidservant of the Lord! Let it be to me according to your word." And the angel departed from her. (Luke 1:26-38)

Through the centuries there has been a great deal of misunderstanding about Mary. On one hand, she is placed on a pedestal. Some would even say we should pray to her and through her to Jesus, which, of course, the Scripture does not teach. But on the other hand, some simply ignore her or misunderstand her place in this greatest of stories.

We need to strip away some of the traditional trappings of Christmas to see Mary's true place for what it is. What can we learn from this girl's life?

Mary was a godly girl living in a godless place.
Did you know that it is possible to live a godly life even though you live or work or go to school in an ungodly environment? Mary proved that. Where did she live? Nazareth.

Nazareth, along with Bethlehem, has been romanticized by believers down through the years. But what was it really like when Mary and Joseph lived there?

It wasn't what you call a destination resort. Far from it.

If Hollywood had been telling it, or if the Christmas story had been stage-managed by some big public relations firm, Jesus would have been born in Rome. Why? Because Rome was the powerful, sophisticated capital of a world empire. But God didn't choose a girl from Rome. Nor did God choose a girl from Athens, the intellectual and cultural capital of the world. He didn't even choose a girl from Jerusalem, home of the great temple and the spiritual capital of Israel.

He picked a girl living in Nazareth.

Nazareth at that time was overrun by Roman soldiers. It was a place where pagan temples had been raised for the worship of countless false gods. It was a place known for wickedness and sin. Someday, some archaeologist digging through the rubble of ancient Nazareth probably will come across the slogan "What happens in Nazareth stays in Nazareth."

The fact is, Nazareth was one of those places that you pass through when you are on your way to somewhere else! I'm reminded a little of Barstow, California. If you happen to be from Barstow, I mean no offense. It's a nice little spot, and they even have an In-N-Out Burger there. It's a great place to pull off the road and get some gas or check your map or whatever. Most people, however, pass through Barstow on the way to somewhere else. Most people don't go there as a destination. It's out in the middle of the desert. That is what Nazareth was like. It was an obscure, off-the-road kind of place.

Unlike Barstow, however, Nazareth was known for its sin and wickedness. That is why, when Nathanael heard that Jesus was from Nazareth, he said, "Can anything good come out of Nazareth?" (John 1:46).

So as Jesus grew up, He became known as "Jesus of Nazareth."

"Jesus of Jerusalem" would have rolled off the tongue a little nicer. People might have thought, *Well, maybe He has something to say, because He is from a great spiritual center.*

Or if it had been "Jesus of Rome," people might have at least thought, *He probably knows some important people. He's probably very well-connected.*

But "Jesus of Nazareth"? Well, that wasn't very impressive. And it was just a little bit embarrassing.

Nevertheless, God picked Mary and this obscure place to accomplish His purpose. He picked an unknown girl living in an unknown place to bring about the most-known event in human history: the birth of the Lord Jesus Christ.

What do we learn from this? We learn that God seems to go out of His way to pick the most unexpected person to accomplish His goals. He seems to go out of His way to choose the most ordinary individual to do the most extraordinary things.

I like the way Paul said it in 1 Corinthians 1:26-28:

> *Take a good look, friends, at who you were when you got called into this life. I don't see many of "the brightest and the best" among you, not many influential, not many from high-society families. Isn't it obvious that God deliberately chose men and women that the culture overlooks and exploits and abuses, chose these "nobodies" to expose the hollow pretensions of the "somebodies"?* (MSG)

We forget that sometimes—even when we're thinking about the "greats" of the Bible like David, Gideon, or the apostle Peter. We forget they became prominent because of what God did through them, not because they were great in themselves. When God called David, he was a shepherd boy, watching over his dad's flock. He was so lightly regarded in his own family that his father had to be strongly prompted even to acknowledge him. Yet God said that David would be the next king of Israel.

When God chose Gideon, calling him a "mighty man of valor," he was hiding from his enemies in a wine press (Judges 6:12). When God called Simon Peter, he was just a regular working stiff out in a boat, trying to keep his fish business going. Yet the Lord raised him up to be one of the great apostles.

Why does God do this? First Corinthians 1:28-29 provides the answer: "God chose things despised by the world, things counted as nothing at all, and used them to bring to nothing what the world considers important. As a result, no one can ever boast in the presence of God" (NLT).

Here's the point: God can use ordinary people. In fact, God prefers and delights to use people like you and me to get the job done and advance His kingdom. So don't ever think of yourself as a nobody out in the middle of nowhere. God knows exactly who you are and where you are. He cares very deeply about you, and He can use you in ways beyond what you have imagined.

Mary is a prime example. He chose an unknown girl from a poorly regarded place to give birth to the King of kings.

Mary was a genuinely humble girl.

Mary was absolutely surprised (and just a little bit frightened) that the angel Gabriel would greet her as "highly favored one" (Luke 1:28). In verse 29, we read that "when she saw him, she was troubled at his saying, and considered what manner of greeting this was."

A better translation would be: "She was thoroughly shaken, wondering what was behind a greeting like that."

The wording of this verse in some translations has led to

many misunderstandings. In these versions, Gabriel says, "Hail, Mary, full of grace. Our Lord is with you. Blessed are you among women." That has even become a prayer to some. But the truth is, Gabriel is not saying "Hail Mary," as in "Praise Mary." A better translation would simply be "Greetings, Mary" or "Greetings to you, Mary. The Lord is with you." What's more, the angel wasn't saying that grace was emanating from Mary, but that God had extended His grace to her. And what is grace? It is the unmerited favor of God.

Yes, Mary was most blessed among women. There is no question about that. But Mary also was a normal human being and a sinner like everyone else. She was not born of immaculate conception herself; that is taught nowhere in Scripture. Mary, in a joyous psalm of praise that she offered after she realized she would be the mother of the Messiah, said, "My soul magnifies the Lord, and my spirit has rejoiced in God my Savior" (Luke 1:46-47).

In other words, Mary needed a Savior like everyone else.

She was so blown away by the greeting of the powerful angel. Why would an angel of the Lord speak to her in that way? She must have said to herself, *It's so overwhelming! I am to be the one. I will be the fulfillment of prophecy.* Perhaps she quoted Isaiah 7:14 in her mind: "Behold, the virgin shall conceive and bear a Son, and shall call His name Immanuel." And she was going to be that virgin! By the way, the word used here for virgin really does mean *virgin*. If you have a translation that says "handmaiden" or "young woman," that is not correct. She never had been involved sexually with a man.

But then Mary had a question for the angel—and a very logical one under the circumstances: "How will this be . . . since I am a virgin?" (Luke 1:34, NIV).

In other words, "With all due respect, Mr. Gabriel, how could this happen? I have never had sex with a man." Mary was humble and reflective, and after she'd thought about it, she asked the logical question.

Mary wasn't doubting as Zechariah did when he was told he would be the father of John. This question had more to do with biology. She wasn't questioning Gabriel; she was only questioning the methodology. *How does this work?* And because it was an honest, legitimate question, Gabriel answered her: "The Holy Spirit will come upon you, and the power of the Highest will overshadow you; therefore, also, that Holy One who is to be born will be called the Son of God" (verse 35).

Sometimes we ask "How?" questions of God, too. How can I live a godly life in this kind of culture? How can I, as a single person, remain sexually pure and wait for God to bring that right person to me? How can I, as a married person, remain faithful to my spouse, attentive to my kids, honest in my work, and uncompromised in my principles? How can I survive this crisis I'm experiencing right now?

How does it work, Lord? How do I do it?

Gabriel has the answer for Mary—and for us—in verse 37: "For with God nothing will be impossible."

Remember that truth! He will complete the work He has begun in your life.

The angel was saying, "The Holy Spirit will come upon you, Mary." And the Holy Spirit comes upon us as well, doesn't He? In fact, the Bible tells us that we are to be filled with the Holy Spirit (see Ephesians 5:18). We are to be filled and refilled and refilled—every day, every hour, every moment. God will give us the power to do what He has called us to do.

Mary was obedient to God's will for her life.

After absorbing this absolutely stunning news, Mary finally replied, "Behold the maidservant of the Lord! Let it be to me according to your word" (verse 38).

In other words, "It's a done deal, Lord. You just tell me where and when." Did she fully understand all the implications of this? Of course not! But what she did understand, she submitted to.

I love it that she didn't demand a detailed explanation of how it would all play out. She didn't say, "Wait. Wait. Wait. How will this work out? How are we going to get Joseph to go along with it? How is this going to appear to others? And what about this? And what about that?" No, she simply submitted to the word of the Lord.

The term *maidservant* that Mary used to describe herself speaks of a voluntary slave, not a person who has been enslaved against her will. This is a person who goes to another and says, "I want to serve you. I don't care if you pay me. I don't care how hard you work me. I don't care what you tell me to do. I want to become your slave, because I am devoted to you." That is what Mary was saying: "Let it be. I am the maidservant of the Lord."

In our lives, there are many times when we want to know God's will before we will submit to it. We want a detailed explanation and want to read the fine print before we sign on the dotted line.

Sometimes I will say to my son, "Can you do something for me?"

And he will reply, "What?" He says that because he is smart. He doesn't say, "Yes, Dad. Whatever you want, I will do it."

Before he agrees, he wants to know what I'm talking about. If I'm asking him to clean out the garage, he wants to leave room to say, "Well, Dad, I'm kind of busy right now."

The fact is, if you want to know God's will for your life, you need to first surrender yourself to Him—without detailed information. Without a roadmap. Someone has wisely said, "The condition of an enlightened mind is a surrendered heart." It is the man or woman with a surrendered heart who will know the will of God.

Mary did that. She submitted her will to God, in spite of not knowing the details and in spite of the complications.

And there certainly were complications.

Again, sometimes we romanticize this story and don't think of Mary and Joseph as real flesh-and-blood people. Mary was a teenager. Some commentators believe she was as young as twelve or perhaps as old as fourteen. She was a young teen called by God, and now she had the task of giving this account to Joseph, her husband-to-be.

Back in those days, you didn't choose your own mate; your parents chose for you. Most likely, Mary and Joseph were still small children when their parents made the decision they would be a good match. And so she was espoused to Joseph, which meant that one day they would be married. From childhood, he knew who his wife would be, and she knew who her husband would be.

And now she was pregnant and would have to explain this to Joseph.

We are not given her words in Scripture, but I imagine it went something like this: "Joseph, I know this is going to sound strange, but an angel has come to me and told me that I am to be with child by the Holy Spirit and that the Spirit Himself will bring this about. If you can believe it, *I am* the virgin with child in Isaiah 7:14. And you need to know that absolutely nothing else has gone on. I promise you that! Joseph, are you okay with this?"

He wasn't okay with it.

Who would be?

Joseph was heartbroken and made up his mind to divorce Mary quietly and somehow move on with his life. But then he also received an angelic visitation, in a dream, at night. Was it Gabriel? The Bible doesn't say, but the message was clear:

"Joseph, son of David," the angel said, "do not be afraid to take Mary as your wife. For the child within her was conceived by the Holy Spirit. And she will have a son, and you are to name him Jesus, for he will save his people from their sins." (Matthew 1:20-21, NLT)

Because Joseph wanted to do the right and honorable thing, the Lord kept him from doing what would have been the wrong thing—divorcing Mary. Instead, the angel not only reassured Joseph's heart about Mary's faithfulness, but he also gave Joseph a glimpse of the Baby's future and what He would accomplish for His people.

Wrapping up, let's go back to Isaiah 9:6, the well-loved passage we have already considered:

For unto us a Child is born,
Unto us a Son is given . . .
And His name will be called
Wonderful, Counselor, Mighty God,
Everlasting Father, Prince of Peace.

Then the prophet looks even further ahead, peering into the distant future beyond Bethlehem, beyond the cross, in the coming days at the end of time when the Son of God returns to earth to establish His everlasting kingdom:

> *Of the increase of His government and peace*
> *There will be no end,*
> *Upon the throne of David and over His kingdom,*
> *To order it and establish it with judgment and justice*
> *From that time forward, even forever.*
> *The zeal of the Lord of hosts will perform this.* (verse 7)

There were so many players in the Christmas story and so many events that had to fit as perfectly together as the inner workings of a clock: the birth of John the Baptist, who would be the forerunner of the Messiah; the miraculous conception of Jesus in the womb of a young virgin; the kindness and faithfulness of Joseph, who determined to obey the Lord and make the Child his own, no matter what people may have whispered behind his back; the decree of Caesar that took Joseph and his pregnant wife to Bethlehem; and the years of research by the Magi in Babylon that set them on a long journey to find a star and a royal Son.

The zeal of the Lord of hosts accomplished all these things, in spite of anything Satan tried to do to disrupt things. God had set His heart on redeeming His people and providing salvation for you and for me. As difficult as it may be to comprehend, God had you in mind when Jesus was born of the virgin. God had you on His heart when Jesus submitted to a Roman cross and poured out His blood. God had your redemption in His thoughts when He raised Jesus from the dead.

His zeal, His great desire to save you and provide a new and exciting life for you, accomplished it all.

What a Savior!

A TWISTED FAMILY TREE

The song says, "Oh, there's no place like home for the holidays."

I agree. I'd rather be home with my little family at Christmas than anywhere else in the world. But "home for Christmas" also can mean getting together with extended family—relatives you don't see (or have to deal with) very often.

And that can be just a little bit stressful.

Let's face it, we all have weird families. We all have that obnoxious uncle, that strange aunt, those twisted cousins. And Grandpa? Well, let's admit it. He's getting just a little bit crazier every year.

Maybe your parents were divorced, and you also have to contend with half brothers, half sisters, and family members who (if you were honest) don't seem much like family at all. Maybe you have to go visit Mom and her new boyfriend or Dad and his new lady, and it's just a little bit awkward.

Or worse yet, they're all coming to your house, and you have to get the place ready, prepare meals, and find spots for everyone to sleep. The following song was written by my friend Dennis Agajanian's father. He called it "Your Relatives Are Coming to Town."

Well, you'd better give up on Christmas this year.
You haven't a chance with everyone here.
Your relatives are coming to town.

They're bringing their kids to add to your fun.
Staying ten days; you thought it was one.
Your relatives are coming to town.

They will monopolize your bathroom
And take your solitude.
They will eat you out of house and home
And complain about your food.

There is only one way to save your Noël:
Give them your home and rent a motel.
Your relatives are coming to town.

This is a time of year when people can become abnormally stressed out. I remember reading in the newspaper about a guy who had dug out his tree lights and was trying to get things sorted out so they could decorate. The problem was, his wife had left the lights in a great big tangled ball the year before, and that made him angry. He set the mess down on the driveway to go into the house for something, and while his back was turned, his teenage daughter pulled into the driveway and drove over the lights.

He freaked out and started screaming at her, "Can't you see I am trying to put up the Christmas lights?"

And then he told his wife he needed to go let off a little bit of steam. So he went into the backyard and started firing off rounds from his 45-caliber pistol. He was arrested for reckless endangerment and ended up in jail (which didn't improve his mood at all).

Not long ago, I read about a man in Rock Springs, Wyoming, who made the mistake of opening his Christmas present too early. Infuriated that he couldn't wait, his wife stabbed him with a kitchen knife.

Ah . . . those family troubles!

Frankly, we all have them. And the person who says they don't is either delusional or outright lying. No one comes from a perfect family, because families are made up of flawed, fallible human beings.

Every now and then I hear people say, "Oh, I came from a dysfunctional home." And I have to bite my tongue to keep from saying, *Will you get over that, already?* We *all* came from dysfunctional homes — every one of us. I came from a dysfunctional home. Now I am the head of a dysfunctional home. What did you expect — that you would have parents like the Cleavers? More likely, they resemble the Simpsons.

Dr. Ian Cook, director of the UCLA Depression Research Program, said this about the Christmas season:

> *Some people have unreasonable expectations — the holidays have to be happy. But if in-laws are sniping at you about your home, your food, and your lifestyle; your two-year-old has already broken his new toys and is wailing . . . happiness can be a tall order.*[1]

Sometimes at Christmas we are presented with ideal pictures of ideal families sitting together in ideal living rooms, watching the snow fall outside and singing carols together. And then we feel like we have fallen short because our family just doesn't look like that. Well, guess what? No one's does. Very few families today even slightly resemble the old movies. But that doesn't mean we can't build some good memories.

The fact is, none of us has the perfect family. Every family has its share of problems, skeletons, dysfunctions, weird dynamics, and eccentric relatives.

It's popular these days to go digging into your family tree, maybe using one of those handy computer programs that assists you in chasing down all the roots, branches, and twigs. I have a friend who's really into this, and every time I see him, he has made some new discovery about his heritage that he wants to tell me about.

There is nothing wrong with pursuing this as a hobby, as long as you remember it works both ways. You might discover that you're related to some famous person or general or president. And you also might find out that your great-grandma was a madam or your grandfather's uncle was hung as a horse thief.

The human family has as many bad apples as good ones. Probably more!

So what if you were researching your ancestors online and discovered that you had a number of prostitutes populating your family tree? Is that something you would want to tell people about?

Your friend might say, "Hey, I found out that I'm a direct descendent of George Washington."

Another friend might counter, "Well, I found out that I have royal blood flowing in my family."

And you would say, "I discovered that we have three prostitutes in our family tree."

Is that something you would be proud of?

Why do I bring that up? Because as we begin to delve into the most famous family tree in human history—the family tree of Jesus Christ Himself—we find liars, cheats, adulterers, and prostitutes. The Lord's family tree has some of the most notable sinners ever, so He knows all about having relatives that might embarrass you. Jesus knows all about dysfunctional family situations. So if you think you are alone in having problems this Christmas, you can know for sure that is simply not the case.

But we will also see something else at work in the family tree of our Lord: grace—incredible, restoring, wonderful grace—the unmerited favor of God.

Why do I bring this up? Because sometimes you and I might look at our lives, sigh deeply, shake our heads, and say, "I don't think God could ever use me. I've made too many mistakes, and I don't see how anything good could come out of the mess I've made of my life."

This story, among other things, shows that is simply not the case. The grace of God is clearly on display here.

The Story Before the Story

When we tell the Christmas story, we usually cut to the chase. By that I mean we go to the beautiful narratives found in Matthew, and especially in Luke, and we revel at the story of the birth of Jesus. When we do that, we often skip over the information that precedes the story. And what precedes the story in the gospel of Matthew is a lengthy list of names—a genealogy.

Why do we skip it? For one thing, the Jewish names sound strange to our ears and are difficult to pronounce. For another thing, it simply doesn't mean that much to us; it doesn't seem to relate to our lives.

Genealogies were a big deal to the Jewish people for a number of reasons. Through these long lists of ancestral names, a family could determine whether they were related to anyone in the priesthood or someone who happened to be in the royal line. The genealogy might also figure into family inheritance issues. So the Jews loved those long lists of names, dating them back as far as they could go.

The genealogy in Matthew 1, however, affects every one of us. What's more, it is as inspired by God as any other passage in the entire Bible. Let's dip into it together:

> *The book of the genealogy of Jesus Christ, the Son of David, the Son of Abraham:*
>
> *Abraham begot Isaac, Isaac begot Jacob, and Jacob begot Judah and his brothers. Judah begot Perez and Zerah by Tamar, Perez begot Hezron, and Hezron begot Ram. Ram begot Amminadab, Amminadab begot Nahshon, and Nahshon begot Salmon. Salmon begot Boaz by Rahab, Boaz begot Obed by Ruth, Obed begot Jesse, and Jesse begot David the king.*
>
> *David the king begot Solomon by her who had been the wife of Uriah. (verses 1–6)*

The mother referred to in that last verse is Bathsheba. Now, drop down to verse 13:

> *Zerubbabel begot Abiud, Abiud begot Eliakim, and Eliakim begot Azor. Azor begot Zadok, Zadok begot Achim, and Achim begot Eliud. Eliud begot Eleazar, Eleazar begot Matthan, and Matthan begot Jacob. And Jacob begot Joseph the husband of Mary, of whom was born Jesus who is called Christ. (verses 13–16)*

When you take the time to look into it, you discover there are some pretty amazing names in this lineup. Normally, Jewish genealogies didn't include women. But in this genealogy, there are *five*. When you find out who some of these people were and what they did, it begins to read like a biblical soap opera. As I said, it certainly gives hope to those of us who have experienced disappointing failures in our lives. In this genealogy, the prelude to the Christmas story, we see God in His mercy doing for sinners what they never could do for themselves. We see the love and grace of God mending broken lives and gently piecing together shattered hopes.

This is why Jesus came.

Some people think Jesus came to earth to make good people just a little bit better or to give us a cause to celebrate and experience deeper happiness and peace. Those are fine things, and the Lord certainly can accomplish such outcomes in our lives.

But that is not why He came.

The reason He came is because we were irreparably separated from God by our sin. As the apostle Paul wrote, we were "without hope and without God in the world."[2] The message of the coming Savior was "You shall call His name Immanuel, for He will save His people from their sins." Christmas is about God's solution for sin. Jesus didn't come to earth to make good people better but to reach out to people who have made a mess of their lives. Jesus came to heal broken lives and to restore shattered hopes.

The book of Galatians tells us,

When the right time came, God sent his Son, born of a woman, subject to the law. God sent him to buy freedom for us who were slaves to the law, so that he could adopt us as his very own children. And because we are his children, God has sent the Spirit of his Son into our hearts, prompting us to call out, "Abba, Father." (4:4-6, NLT)

Jesus came to redeem us.

Don't let that word *redeem* throw you. It simply means "to buy back" and was used for an individual who would buy back a slave who was up for auction in the slave market.

That is what Jesus did. He saw us in the slave market of sin, paid the price for our freedom, and set us free from the power of sin and the ultimate penalty of sin. That is the *real* message of Christmas.

Jesus came to put broken lives back together. As He began His ministry, He stood in the synagogue of His hometown, Nazareth, and read these words of Scripture, pertaining to Himself:

The Spirit of the LORD *is upon Me,*
Because He has anointed Me
To preach the gospel to the poor,
He has sent Me to heal the brokenhearted
To proclaim liberty to the captives
And recovery of sight to the blind,
To set at liberty those who are oppressed. (Luke 4:18)

Jesus has come to heal your broken your heart.

Do you have a broken heart? Do you have a shattered life? Do you have a mess on your hands, and you can't blame anyone but yourself? Or could it be that you are living in a mess created by someone else, and it seems so unfair? Jesus has come to put these things back together again.

The gospel of Matthew emphasizes the fact that Jesus fulfilled the prophecies of the Old Testament concerning the coming Messiah. Part of the evidence Matthew used to demonstrate that fact is the genealogy in the first chapter, which traces Jesus' lineage to the royal line of David. Why is that important? Because the Bible said the Messiah would come out of the root and offspring of David. Any claimant to the throne of Israel had to demonstrate, through his genealogy, that he descended from David and was in the line of royalty.

Two genealogies are given to us in the gospels: one in Matthew and the other in Luke. These represent Jesus' paternal genealogy

(Matthew) and his maternal genealogy (Luke). In other words, Matthew's genealogy traces Jesus through Joseph's line, while Luke traces it through Mary's ancestry. And both trace back to David.

That is why Mary and Joseph had to go to Bethlehem to pay the tax demanded by Caesar. Bethlehem was the boyhood home of David before he ascended the throne. It was a legal necessity for them to return to David's ancestral home to pay their tax, but it also was a direct fulfillment of Micah 5:2:

> But you, Bethlehem Ephrathah,
> Though you are little among the thousands of Judah,
> Yet out of you shall come forth to Me
> The One to be Ruler in Israel,
> Whose goings forth are from of old,
> From everlasting.

It's important to notice that Matthew doesn't refer to Joseph as the father of Jesus. The text refers to him as "the husband of Mary, of whom was born Jesus who is called Christ" (1:16). Scripture is abundantly clear in pointing out that Jesus was not the son of Joseph. Joseph was the husband of Mary and became a father figure and a guardian to Jesus. Jesus' Father is literally God, who caused the birth of our Lord to take place supernaturally in the womb of the virgin by the power of the Holy Spirit.

Because Jesus had no human father, He couldn't be a descendent of David, except through His mother. Be that as it may, the legal right to rule always came through the father's side. In Jesus' case, He was legally Joseph's oldest son.

Interesting Characters on the Family Tree

David

Plucked from obscurity, David became the greatest king in Israel's history. God Himself called David "a man after My own heart" (Acts 13:22). His name is usually associated with two other names that describe both his greatest victory and his greatest, most tragic defeat.

On the victory side, who could forget Goliath, the nine-foot-six Philistine warrior David killed in the Valley of Elah with only a sling and a stone? I was telling this story to my granddaughter not long ago and showing her how Goliath fell. I said, "You be David," which of course meant she got to throw the stone—only we didn't use stones, we used pillows. So I fell forward, just like Goliath, and crashed on the bed. Then she was the giant, and I got to be David and smack her with the pillow. (I'm sure it was all very instructive for her.)

Goliath was David's greatest victory.

On the defeat side, we remember the sorrow and anguish caused by David's adultery with Bathsheba, the wife of his loyal warrior and friend, Uriah the Hittite. David not only stole a man's wife, but he also stole the man's life. He deliberately had Uriah killed in battle in an attempt to cover up his sin with Bathsheba and the resulting pregnancy.

Yet the royal line originates with David, and Jesus Himself would be called "the Son of David" (Matthew 1:1). Despite his sin, David made it into the most exclusive family tree in human history.

Abraham

In Matthew 1:2, we read about Abraham, a very great man in Jewish history who is considered the father of the Jews and the father of the faith. But he also had flaws and shortcomings. We know that he lied (twice) about the identity of his wife, Sarah, trying to pass her off as his sister. He did it because she was a beautiful woman, and Abraham wanted to protect his own skin in case a powerful ruler went after her. This demonstrated not only deception and cowardice but also a lack of faith in the God who had called him and led him through the land of Canaan.

In spite of these things, God established Abraham as the father of the Jewish people and put him clearly in the Messianic line.

Tamar

How in the world did this woman end up in the Lord's family tree? Quite honestly, I'm surprised by that. Her sordid story is told in Genesis 38. As you read her story of prostitution and deception, you will be hard-pressed to find anything of redeeming value. She is pretty much a corrupt character, without much of a silver lining. Yet amazingly, by the grace of God, she ends up being an ancestress of the Messiah Himself.

Rahab

Speaking of prostitutes, Tamar had to play the part of a prostitute once, to obtain her goal. But Rahab was a regular professional. Her house of ill repute was known by everyone in the city of Jericho. Tamar resorted to prostitution to obtain a certain end, but Rahab did it for money. What's more, she also was a Gentile, a Canaanite. When the Israelite army sent spies into Jericho to scope out the city before an impending attack, Rahab hid them in her home and was subsequently blessed as a result.

We speak of "Rahab the harlot," and somehow that doesn't sound so bad. But we could also say, "Rahab the prostitute." That is what she was. Yet because she did this act of kindness toward the people of God, she and her family were spared when Jericho was conquered. Even more surprising, she was brought into the messianic line as the wife of Salmon and the mother of the godly Boaz—David's great-grandfather.

Ruth

Like Tamar and Rahab, Ruth was a Gentile. She married one of two sons born to a woman named Naomi. They were both Jewish boys, Mahlon and Chilion, whose names meant "sickly" and "pining." True to their names, both of these brothers died, leaving two young Moabite widows. Naomi's husband also died.

When brokenhearted Naomi decided to return to Israel from the land of Moab, she told her two widowed daughters-in-law they would do better if they stayed in Moab. One of the women took her advice and turned back, but Ruth refused to leave Naomi's side. When the older woman tried to send her away, Ruth spoke words that would go down in history:

> *Entreat me not to leave you,*
> *Or to turn back from following after you;*
> *For wherever you go, I will go;*
> *And wherever you lodge, I will lodge;*
> *Your people shall be my people,*
> *And your God, my God. (Ruth 1:16)*

It was a wonderful affirmation of Ruth's loyal heart. But what makes it all so remarkable is that Ruth was a Moabite, a woman of Moab, one of Israel's worst enemies. Where did the Moabites come from? They were the result of the incestuous relations of Lot with his two unmarried daughters. The son produced by Lot's union with his older daughter was Moab, the father of the Moabites.

It starts to sound like some tacky reality show on TV. And yet here is this pagan woman from Moab, Israel's ancestral enemy, who comes to faith in God and marries Boaz. In so doing, she becomes the grandmother of David, Israel's greatest king.

Bathsheba

It's interesting to note that in Matthew's genealogy, Bathsheba is identified only as "the wife of Uriah" (1:6). Even in the Messianic line, though she is included, we are reminded that she was the wife of another. David the king begot Solomon by "her who had been the wife of Uriah."

Some commentators place all the blame on David for that affair with Bathsheba, but I think she comes in for a share of blame as well. As they say, "It takes two to tango," and maybe she shouldn't have been bathing in plain sight of the palace, where David could see her. After the sin took place, she also cooperated in the cover-up that went on for a long period of time.

Even so, God extended His grace to her and included her in the Messianic line.

To me, that is one of the great values of the first chapter of Matthew. We can look at the names of the people listed in the Messianic line and be blown away by the grace of God. This is a God who can take the darkest, most twisted, and unhappy life stories and bring something good out of them for His glory. No matter what your family background is or how you came into being, God has a plan and a purpose for your life.

Let me illustrate: The McDaniel clan, my family on my

mother's side, originally came from Scotland, settling mostly in Arkansas. And then some of them, including my mother, came out to California. As I mentioned earlier, I was born out of wedlock. I was the result of a one-night stand that my mom had with some sailor she met in Long Beach.

I don't have a beautiful family tree that I can point to. Looking back on my McDaniel ancestors, it seems like they were either notorious sinners or notorious Christians. We have a lot of alcoholics and more than our share of tragedy in our family background. And my father's background? I don't even know what it is, because I don't know my father.

So here I am, not planned and conceived out of wedlock. Yet *God* had a plan for my life, and He chose me to be His child. And He has a plan for your life as well.

I am a child of God today because of God's grace. Period. The Bible says,

> *For by grace you have been saved through faith, and that not of yourselves; it is the gift of God, not of works, lest anyone should boast. For we are His workmanship, created in Christ Jesus for good works, which God prepared beforehand that we should walk in them. (Ephesians 2:8-10)*

We are reminded that even if we fail like Abraham or David, like Rahab or Tamar or Bathsheba, there is still hope. God can take the broken pieces of our lives and put them back together.

Maybe your life is in something of a mess right now. Your family might be falling apart, or perhaps you have sinned in some area of your life. Know that God can take this mess and bring about transformation. He can turn the broken pieces into something beautiful: a masterpiece.

What Do We Learn from the Genealogy of Jesus?
We see the grace of God richly displayed.

The stories of these four women on the list in Matthew 1 aren't included so you can focus on their sin; they are included so you can marvel over the incomparable grace of God. Yes, other Scriptures describe their shortcomings in detail. But they are included in *this* list to show God's kindness and grace being extended.

That doesn't mean we should minimize or celebrate sin or imagine that we can disobey God without facing consequences. As the apostle Paul said in Romans 6, "What shall we say, then? Shall we go on sinning so that grace may increase [or overflow, or literally go down the drain]? By no means! We died to sin; how can we live in it any longer?" (verses 1-2, NIV).

Everyone faces repercussions for their sin. David faced repercussions. So did Tamar. Nevertheless, we are reminded that God truly is a forgiving God and will give us a second chance to obey Him and serve Him. That is the grace of God on display.

Maybe you have made some wrong choices, too. You need to come to the Lord and say, "Father, I have failed. Would You redeem those failures? Will You redeem my life and bring something good, something of value, in spite of the wrong I have done?"

He has done that over and over again for millions of people, and He will do it for you.

The focus is on Jesus, not on His family.

As I look at the Lord's family and His ancestors, I say to myself, *Wow. His family was messed up like mine is.* But the effect of looking at these failing, fallible people in the Lord's family tree also causes me to say, *This is a God who is approachable. This is a God who can understand where I come from and what I struggle with. This is a God I can know.*

For many people today, the God of the Bible seems too good to be true. Jesus seems like a one-dimensional figure in stained glass a million miles from real life, with all its pains and troubles and complications.

When I was a little boy, I went to live with my grandparents for a time, and I accompanied my grandmother to church on Sunday. I didn't understand most of what I heard and saw. But I remember that in my grandmother's home, she had a painting of Jesus—a familiar depiction of Him that was very popular in the 1950s. I'm sure you've seen it, and you may even have it in your home. In this particular depiction of Christ, He is turned away, looking somewhere off into the distance. He's not looking at you; His attention is elsewhere.

I remember looking at that picture of Jesus and thinking to myself, *I would like to know that Jesus — but I don't think I can know Him. Besides, He isn't interested in me. He isn't even looking at me in the picture.*

That is how I felt about God — that He was busy, preoccupied, and didn't really care about someone like Greg Laurie. Maybe you have thought of God as angry or disappointed in you — someone who is always ready to come down on you because you don't measure up.

Both of those impressions are false.

The authentic flesh-and-blood Jesus of the Bible was in touch with the real world. He came from a real family with lots of problems, yet He Himself was without sin.

Jesus became a part of the human family so that we might become a part of the heavenly family. He has walked in your shoes and understands your life situation better than you know it yourself (no matter how twisted and complicated it may seem to you).

Though Jesus was without sin Himself, He loved sinners. In fact, His enemies called Him "the friend of sinners." (And I don't think He minded that at all.) He was tested in all points as we are, and yet He was without sin. Hebrews 7:25 tells us that "he is able, once and forever, to save those who come to God through him. He lives forever to intercede with God on their behalf" (NLT).

We can have hope for our future and the future of our families.

While you may not have murderers or prostitutes in your family tree, you surely have some adulterers, liars, and cheats. No family would be complete without them. But Jesus can intervene in your life, just as it is.

Allow me to offer this word of caution: It has been said that an ounce of prevention is better than a ton of cure. What state is your family in right now? If you are the man of the family, are you a good spiritual leader? I have found, in far too many Christian homes, that the woman—the wife and mother—is the spiritual leader, the initiator of all things spiritual. She is the one who says, "Come on, it's Sunday. Let's get up and go to church. Let's get going." Or she will be the one to say, "Let's read a little bit of Scripture together." Or perhaps, "Let's pray about this. Let's take it to the Lord." All too often, it is the man—the husband and father—who drags his feet or finds an excuse not to do those things.

In many cases, then, the man is passive at best about spiritual things. In some situations, he actually drags his family down, saying things like "I don't want to go to church. Why don't you stay home with me?"

That is the reminder this family tree in Scripture gives me. Someday, someone will be looking at your place in the family. Will they just skip over your name, as if you weren't even there or had no influence at all? Or, will they pause by your name and say, "This was a godly man. This man loved the Lord and encouraged his family in the Lord."

If you are the man of the house, what I am saying right now is to step up and take some spiritual initiative and leadership.

"Well, Greg," you say, "it's too late for that. I've made a lot of mistakes and missed a lot of opportunities." Welcome to the club! So have all of us. As long as you are drawing breath, however, it's not too late to have an influence on your loved ones by the example you set. God bless your wife and thank the Lord for her interest in spiritual things. But it's time for you to be a man and take some spiritual leadership. It's time for you to love your wife as Christ loves His church (see Ephesians 5:25-33).

If you are a wife reading these words, you're not off the hook! You are to love and respect your husband. When was the last time you told him how much you appreciate everything he does for you and for the family? He knows the things you don't like about him and where you think he's falling short. Maybe it's time you affirmed him as the spiritual leader in your home. When he takes even a baby step in that direction, respond with encouragement.

What kind of parent are you right now? Are you raising your children in the training and instruction of the Lord (see

Ephesians 6:1-4)? You should be able to say to your sons and daughters, "Not only live by what I teach you, *but live the way that I live.* Do what I do."

News flash: You will fall short and make mistakes. When you do, it's good to go to your kids and say, "Guess what? Dad blew it" or "Mom fell short" or "I made a mistake" or "I was out of bounds just now, and I want to ask for your forgiveness." Does this mean you will lose some authority and respect by humbling yourself like that? No, you will gain their respect as you show them how a man of God or a woman of God owns up to mistakes and relies on the Lord for help. In fact, your children will model your behavior and be more willing to admit faults and ask for forgiveness as well.

It is so tragic when we see the sins of the parents visited on the children and the bad behavior of one generation being picked up by the next one and the next one and the next. That certainly happens, and we can all point to examples in our own experience. Nevertheless, the Lord can step in, intervene, and change things—if we give Him that opportunity.

Maybe you have a prodigal son or daughter. My own son Christopher, now with the Lord, didn't always walk with Christ, though he was raised in a Christian home by parents who loved him with all their hearts. There was a time for a number of years when Christopher went astray. He never stopped believing in God, and he never was disrespectful to his mother or me. He just went his own way. At one point, after he came back to the Lord, he said to a friend of mine, "One of the reasons I came back again was because I knew that my parents loved me unconditionally." Later, he recommitted his life to Christ and became a Christian husband and father.

If you have children who have gone astray, just let them know that you love them. And keep the porch light on and the door open. Perhaps God, in His mercy, would even use this Christmas season to bring about some reconciliation in your home—if not this year, then perhaps next. Keep praying, and keep holding on to hope.

Sons and daughters are part of that family tree and have responsibilities as well. Ephesians 6:1-3 says, "Children, obey your parents in the Lord, for this is right. 'Honor your father and mother . . . that it may go well with you'" (NIV). If you are a son—even an adult son—when did you last call your mother? If you are a daughter, when is the last time you let your dad know how much you appreciate him?

We all have our part to play in the family tree.

Sometimes Christmas, with all its family pressure, is the time when some of our relationship problems come to the surface. So be it! Instead of running from those difficulties or trying to sweep them under the rug, you need to bring the matters before the Lord and then, with His help, deal with them. Why not let Christmas be a time of healing and new closeness rather than tension and unhappiness?

Your marriage, of course, is your most important relationship beside your relationship with God. Is it holding strong? Fraying around the edges? Beginning to unravel? If you have even contemplated divorce, let me plead with you: Don't get a divorce. Reconcile. Give it another chance. Remember that your decision will not only affect your lives alone, but also the lives of the generations that follow you.

Are you a single person? Remain pure. Don't start a family unintentionally. Wait for the right man or the right woman whom God has prepared for you. And if you have messed up, come to the Lord and say, "Lord, here it is. Here is my mistake. Here is my sin. Here is my shortcoming. I am asking You to redeem these things, Lord. I am asking You to intervene. I am asking You to bring beauty out of ashes, as only You can." Then, watch what the Lord can do.

If you struggle with doubts about how He can work, look again at His own family tree. Remember Rahab the prostitute; Tamar, who seduced her own father-in-law; and David, who committed adultery and took the life of a loyal friend. If the Lord could redeem these situations, bringing back all of those names to a position of honor and blessing, He can do the same thing in your family tree as well.

✳ ✳ ✳ ✳ ✳ ✳ ✳ ✳ ✳ ✳ ✳ ✳ ✳ ✳

PART 2

CHRISTMAS LOST AND FOUND

5

DON'T MISS CHRISTMAS

So many people completely miss the point of Christmas.

The truth is, Christmas has been hijacked by secular culture and emptied of its meaning. There is so much fantasy and myth imposed on this holiday that people have become numb to the real miracle of Christ's birth.

I heard the story of a lady who took her little boy to Sunday school for the first time, where he heard the story of our Lord's birth. It was all new to him. He had never heard anything like it.

When he got home, he excitedly described it all to his mom.

"Mom," he said, "today I learned about the very first Christmas in Sunday school. There wasn't a Santa Claus back then, but there were these three skinny guys on camels that had to deliver all the toys. And Rudolph, the red-nosed reindeer with his nose so bright, wasn't there yet, so they had to have this big spotlight from the sky to guide these three skinny guys around."

That's a pretty good illustration of how our reference point has changed as a culture. Many of our children start with the shallow Christmas myths, but don't know anything about the real, historical account that launched everything—the greatest story of all.

In all the madness that accompanies this season, we can actually miss Christmas. You say, "Greg, it's not possible to miss Christmas. My Sunday newspaper weighs in at about thirty pounds because it is stuffed with ads pressuring me to buy stuff. The TV is reminding me. The radio is reminding me. Even when I go on the Internet, there are those obnoxious little pop-up ads that remind me. To tell you the truth, I'm worn out by it all."

I'm reminded of a story I heard about a mother who was running furiously from store to store on Christmas Eve to get those last-minute gifts. Suddenly she realized that she had lost her three-year-old son. In a panic, she retraced her steps and found her little guy with his nose pressed up against a frosty window, gazing at a manger scene.

When he heard his mother shout out his name, he said, "Mommy, Mommy, look! It's the baby Jesus in the hay!"

The stressed-out mom grabbed him and jerked him away, saying, "We don't have time for that. Can't you see that Mommy is trying to get ready for Christmas?"

That is how it can be. Because of all the clutter of Xmas—and

I use that term intentionally—we forget about the Christ of Christmas. So come back to the manger of Bethlehem, and Christmas will come alive to you.

"Who's Responsible for This?"

A woman was doing some last-minute Christmas shopping at a crowded mall. She was tired of fighting the crowds and standing in lines and getting all those gifts and so forth. Finally, almost done with her shopping, she pushed the elevator button, the door opened, and it was packed with people.

Have you ever had that moment? Everyone looks at you with an expression that says, "Don't come in here." But you really don't want to wait any longer, because you have already waited a long time. So she wedged her way into the packed elevator.

As they were on their way down, she just couldn't hold in her frustrations any longer. Breaking all the rules of elevator decorum, she suddenly blurted out, "Whoever is responsible for this whole Christmas thing ought to be arrested, strung up, and shot!"

A few others nodded in agreement. And then, from the back of the elevator, came a single voice that said, "Don't worry. They already crucified Him."

Now Jesus is certainly not responsible for the madness of Christmas. He wasn't born that we might shop; He was born to die that we might live. There was no room for Him at the inn. In fact, it seems the only place where there was room for Him was on the cross.

But often those who are conversant with spiritual truth are in the greatest danger of indifference. If you are in a good Bible-teaching church, you are blessed with the privilege of hearing the Word of God taught day in and day out. But there is a danger that comes with such a blessing. If you listen to those truths with a wrong heart, with no intention of applying what you have heard, if you're just going through the motions, your heart actually can grow hard to the things of God.

If contact with holy things does not convert or change your heart, it can cause your heart to become jaded and cynical. We can become indifferent or flippant about the tender story of the Nativity. We can become jaded to the message of the gospel, because we have heard it so many times. As so many through the years have affirmed, familiarity breeds contempt.

Don't let that happen to you. Keep a tender and open heart toward God. Don't let religion crowd out Jesus. Don't miss Christmas.

Make time for Jesus. Make room for Jesus. I love the Christmas hymn *Joy to the World* because one of the lines says, "Let every heart prepare Him room."

Make room for Him this year.

In Honor of the King

Maybe you have heard the story about the man who went to a garage sale and noticed something under a tarp in the back of the garage. Pulling the tarp back, he saw that it was an old, classic Harley Davidson motorcycle.

The bike didn't seem to be part of the sale, but the man thought to himself that it wouldn't do any harm to ask the owner, an older man, about it.

"Say," he said to the man, "do you want to sell that thing?"

The owner thought for a moment, then shrugged his shoulders. "You know," he said, "I've been meaning to get it fixed up. But I don't think I'll ever get around to it. So I might as well sell it."

"How much do you want for it?"

"Well, if I took it down to the junkyard, they'd probably give me thirty-five bucks for it. Just give me the thirty-five bucks, and you can take it."

So they agreed, and Bob, the man who was buying the motorcycle, loaded it in his truck and took it home. For several months, he let the old bike sit in his own garage, under a tarp, just like the old man had. But then he said to himself, *I need a project. I'm going to put this old Harley back together.*

Getting ready for his project, Bob called the local Harley dealer to check on a few major parts he would need to restore the bike. The Harley guy asked for the serial number of the bike, which Bob gave to him. Suddenly, the man on the other end of the line sounded different—maybe a little excited. He said, "Can I get your name, address, and phone number? I'll call you right back."

Bob gave him the information, but then he felt kind of jittery after he had hung up the phone. *What was that all about?* he wondered. *Maybe some Hell's Angel owned the bike, and it was involved in some kind of crime. Or maybe it was stolen!*

A couple of hours went by, and Bob got a call. The man on the other end of the line identified himself as an executive with Harley Davidson Motorcycles, and he had a strange request.

"I'd like you to do something for me, Bob. Don't hang up, but I'd like you to go over to the bike, take the seat off of it, and turn it over. Tell me if anything is written there." Bob complied with the instructions, picked up the phone again, and said, "Yeah, the words 'The King' are written on the seat."

There was a brief pause on the line, and then the man from Harley Davidson said, "Bob, I am prepared to offer you $300,000 cash for that motorcycle right now. Do we have a deal?"

"No," Bob answered, "we don't have a deal. I need to find out what's going on here."

An hour later, he got a call from a Hollywood celebrity, who was a collector of old cars and motorcycles. The celebrity offered Bob $500,000 for the bike. Bob later found out that his newly acquired Harley originally belonged to Elvis Presley, "the King of

Rock and Roll." It had been lost for years, and now that it had been rediscovered, it was a thing of great value.

An urban legend? Possibly. But it makes a point: That which was in the back of a garage under a tarp, purchased for $35 and thought of as having no value, had suddenly become very valuable because of who had owned that old Harley and ridden it.

At Christmastime, we celebrate the birth of the King—the real King, the King of the Jews and the King of the universe, Christ the Messiah, our Savior. But like that old Harley, His birth wasn't noted or valued at the time. For the most part, people missed that first Christmas.

They still do.

I remember reading an article in the newspaper about a man who had a nativity scene set up in his front yard. You know the typical scene: Mary and Joseph, the little Baby Jesus, and a few sheep thrown in. All of these figures had little lights in them.

One night, some vandals came along and stole his plastic Baby Jesus with a ten-watt bulb inside. This guy got really stressed out about it. The local newspaper interviewed him, and in the article he pleaded with the robbers to "please bring Jesus back to me."

I read that and thought, *You know what, buddy? Maybe you need to get a life. We're talking a plastic replica here.* But to him, that was really important.

In a broad sense, you might say that this man was looking for Jesus. Unfortunately, his Jesus was a plastic baby with a light bulb inside. But at least he thought enough of Jesus to miss the plastic replica. Many other people at this time of year are working feverishly to remove any remembrance of Jesus from public view.

These are generally the same people who have tried to remove the phrase "one nation under God" from our Pledge of Allegiance, labored tirelessly to keep prayer out of our schools, gone to court to keep anyone from seeing the Ten Commandments posted in public view, and generally done everything they could to remove the name of Jesus Christ—or even the word *Christmas*—from their no-name holiday celebrations.

In Portland, Maine, a site manager for that city's housing authority recently attempted to clarify a new policy that banned all religious celebrations or decorations. It mandated, "There shall be no angels, crosses, Stars of David, or any other icons of religion displayed on the walls, floors, ceilings, et cetera, of your apartment buildings, except within your own apartment." The dictum went on to decree that anything hanging on the inside of the resident's door was permissible, but nothing whatsoever was allowed on the outside, exposed to the hallway, because "it might offend someone."

Or how about the grade school principal in Sacramento, California, who strictly warned his teachers against using the word *Christmas* on any written materials within their classrooms?

In case you haven't noticed, the new politically correct greeting this time of the year is no longer "Merry Christmas," but the more generic, insipid "Happy Holidays."

I refuse to say Happy Holidays.

My recommendation? Say "Merry Christmas" to people—cheerfully, distinctly, politely, and without shame! Or when you receive one of those wimpy "Happy Holidays" greetings, smile your brightest smile and say, "Why, thank you! And God bless you" or "Jesus loves you." We who belong to Jesus ought to have no shame in declaring His name or His love. We *own* Him in public, just as He owns us.

The attempt to remove every vestige of Christmas, however, has gone to almost unbelievable lengths. Now even the humble *snowflake* has been deemed offensive. In Saratoga Springs, New York, third graders at Division Street Elementary School saw their Christmas project confiscated by an indignant principal. Entering their classroom, he was struck with horror when he saw the boys and girls adorning an oversized Christmas ornament with colored photos of snowflakes. He quickly removed the offending item from sight, and there is no word as to whether the teacher was allowed to keep her job. (She probably had to attend sensitivity training.)

Others have banned poinsettias for alleged "religious connotations."

All of this seems incredibly sad to me.

But when you think about it, there is something even sadder than that. There are sincere believers in the Lord Jesus Christ who will lose sight of Him this year, during the very season that was set apart to honor His entry into our world.

Missing Person

Have you ever felt as though you somehow lost God from your life? One day as you were going about your affairs, you suddenly realized that something was missing. And that's when it dawned on you that you hadn't given a single thought to God all day or maybe for several days. That connection with heaven you had always enjoyed seemed distant at best. It was almost as though He were gone.

I heard the story of a little boy who wandered into a local church. Wide-eyed, he saw all the candles lit for a time of prayer. Misunderstanding the meaning of those symbols, he proceeded to blow out all the candles and sing "Happy Birthday" to Jesus.

The minister, who observed all this, was incensed. When the boy walked out the doors, he followed him home. After the little guy went into his house, the minister knocked on the door, and the boy's mother answered.

"Yes, Reverend, what can I do for you?"

He replied, "Ma'am, I want to speak with your son. He has no respect for God whatsoever."

With a sigh, she said, "Okay, come on in. I'll get him."

The little boy walked slowly down the stairs from his room, coming to stand in front of the stern-faced man of the cloth.

"I have a question for you, son," he said. "Where is *God*?"

The boy didn't know what to say.

Again, the minister leaned forward and said, "Little boy, I asked you a question. *Where is God?*" At this, the boy's eyes went wide as saucers, and he started to tremble. When the minister asked him one more time, the little boy bolted out of the room, ran upstairs, and slammed his bedroom door behind him.

His mother ran to his room and said, "Honey, what's wrong?"

"Mommy," her son said in a frightened voice, "they have lost God at that church, and they think I took Him!"

We can lose God in the holiday season. But here is something to consider: If you feel far from God, *guess who moved?* God hasn't gone anywhere, but maybe we have. And in the busyness of the season and in the so-called celebration of the birth of Christ, we can forget all about Him.

You know how it is. On Wednesday there's a white elephant gift exchange at the office. Then on Thursday, there's that special Christmas movie you wanted to see with the family. And the weekend? Yikes! You haven't sent Christmas cards yet, and there's so much shopping. How will you ever get it all done?

And somewhere in it all, we lose track of our Lord.

Maybe there was a point in your life when you walked closely with the Lord, but in recent days, it seems as though you have lost sight of Him.

A Lost Love

I'm reminded of the words of Jesus to the church of Ephesus in Revelation 2:

> *I know your deeds, your hard work and your perseverance. I know that you cannot tolerate wicked men, that you have tested those who claim to be apostles but are not, and have found them false. You have persevered and have endured hardships for my name, and have not grown weary.*
>
> *Yet I hold this against you: You have forsaken your first love. Remember the height from which you have fallen! Repent and do the things you did at first. If you do not repent, I will come to you and remove your lampstand from its place. (verses 2-5, NIV)*

To read this account, it sounds as though the First Church of Ephesus was a busy, active, productive church. They wouldn't tolerate false teaching, and they seemed to have all their doctrinal ducks in a row.

But somehow, in all that activity, work, and study, they had lost sight of Jesus. And the Lord Himself had to say to them, "You have left your first love."

Work had taken the place of worship. Perspiration had taken the place of inspiration. So the Great Physician, our Lord Himself, wrote them a prescription for renewal, or revival: *Remember from where you have fallen. Repent and do the first works quickly.* I sum it up with the three Rs for getting right with God: *remember, repent,* and *repeat.*

"Get Back"

Maybe there was a time when you were closer to God, but now, for whatever reason, you're not in that place. You can remember what it was like. You read one of your old journals, and it just overflows with love for Jesus. But now there's a distance.

What do you do? In the immortal words of Paul, John, George, and Ringo, "Get back, get back, get back to where you once belonged." In other words, remember where you were, and go back to that place.

Do you remember the way it was when you first came to Jesus Christ? Do you remember the passion, the excitement?

I saw a movie recently that included the testimonies of a group of young surfers who had all come to Christ. It was so refreshing to hear the stories of these young men who had come out of a life of partying and drugs and all that other stuff that young kids get themselves into.

Then one of them came to Christ and started telling all his friends about the Lord. And one by one, this whole group of friends gave their lives to Christ, and now they are all serving Him.

Some of these guys were very successful in their sport and had lots of honors and accolades thrown their way. They were making money and acquiring some fame. But at the same time, all of them admitted to an emptiness in their lives—an emptiness now filled to overflowing by a relationship with God through Jesus. And they were talking about how thrilling it was to have a Bible study and what a joy it was to pray together.

It reminded me of thousands who have come to Christ through the years of our ministry in places all over the world. There is almost always evidence that something is different, something has changed. There are changed priorities as you seek to know Him better and walk with Him more closely. You look forward to being with other believers at church and at Bible studies and worship times. You're excited about getting alone with God in prayer.

Frankly, if these things don't draw you and excite you, that would tell me there is something spiritually wrong. It would tell me that maybe you need to get back to where you were, where you should be. *Remember* from where you have fallen. *Repent* and change your direction. And *repeat*, doing those things you used to do when Jesus was number one in your life.

It's amazing how we can go through a day and never think about Jesus. In many ways, we can practically live like atheists, with no thought of God whatsoever, except when we get our food: *Oh, yeah. Let's pray. Lord, uh, bless this food.* Hello. Good-bye.

Have you lost sight of Jesus? As we enter a new year, let's make a real effort to remember Him by taking time for the Word of God. And by that I mean carving out time for Bible study. Don't just try to work it into your busy schedule. *Change* your busy schedule and make time for God's Word.

Let's remember Him by taking time each and every day for prayer—a time to spend in the presence of God, listening to His voice as well as baring our hearts to Him and bringing our petitions to Him. Jesus said that men ought always to pray and not give up (see Luke 18:1).

Let's remember Him in our involvement in church, with His people—not just working it in when we can find time, but understanding there is a priority in gathering with God's people for worship and prayer. Church is not just a place where we take in. It is also a place where we give out. It is a place to use the gifts God has given to us, to seek spiritual accountability, and to listen to the advice that others can give to us. It is a place to invest our finances and share in what God is doing.

Remember Him also as you look for opportunities to share your faith with others. The Christmas season is such a natural time to speak about Jesus and to tell others about this One who has been born and was crucified and has risen again from the dead.

Don't miss the *real* Christmas this Christmas.

Looking back into the biblical account, we can identify people or groups of people who certainly did miss the incredible significance of what was happening right in front of them.

First, there was a certain innkeeper . . .

The Innkeeper Missed Christmas

What the tired couple needed when they came into Bethlehem was a nice motel—or just any motel! As they walked through town, however, all they could see were "no vacancy" signs. They came to the inn where they had hoped to stay, but there was no room for them and they were turned away.

Presumably, it was an innkeeper who delivered this bad news. Clearly he could see that Mary was well along in her pregnancy and that she needed a clean and warm room in case she was to give birth.

But he stood at the door of the inn and shook his head. "Sorry," he basically said. "No room. Nothing available."

Frankly, it's hard for me to imagine a man being that heartless. Call me old-fashioned if you like, but I'm one of those people who believes that when a woman is headed toward a door, a man should open that door for her. I know very well that some women don't appreciate that these days, but I think there are still a lot of women who do. And if I'm seated in a train or a bus and a woman walks in with no place to sit, I give her my seat. It's a matter of common courtesy—especially if she is an older woman and certainly if she is a pregnant woman.

I think we should go out of our way to assist an expectant mother because of the discomfort that pregnancy brings. You want to make it a little easier for her.

So I have a difficult time with this innkeeper who turned away an obviously pregnant young woman and her husband. It seems like simple human kindness would say, *Clear a space for these two. Put a roof over them. She could give birth tonight.*

In this woman's womb was the Creator of the universe in human form. And this guy was too busy to give them the time of day, much less a place of rest and shelter.

If you were Joseph, with the responsibility for this woman and the unborn child, you would find yourself saying, *Now what?* As it turned out, there was a ramshackle little building—or perhaps a cave—behind the inn that was used as a stable for the animals. With no other options, it was there that Joseph finally sought shelter for the night.

It's easy to vilify a man like this innkeeper and think of him as a wicked man. That could have been the case. But more plausibly, I think he probably was just a very busy man. Preoccupied with making money, he had all the business he could handle that night and didn't take time to consider "the right thing to do."

It reminds me of our country today and those who have no time to seek God. You invite people to church and they reply, "Well, we're just too busy right now. We have so much to do."

We say, "Why don't you come to church with us on Christmas?"

And we hear replies like "That's a nice idea, but . . . we're going to a play . . . this movie just opened . . . we have to do a bit more shopping . . . we have another commitment."

I'm reminded of the psalmist, who talked about those who couldn't be bothered with seeking the Lord. He wrote, "In all his thoughts there is no room for God."[1]

So it is with many in today's world. Even on the day set aside to celebrate the birth of Jesus Christ, there's no time for Him at all. Nothing left in the schedule. No time for faith. No room in the inn.

So, the Savior of the world was born in a barn. But it wasn't Jesus who missed out; it was the innkeeper. Why did he miss out? Because he was interested in the bottom line: the dollar . . . the buck . . . or, in his case, the shekel. In the busyness of all that was going on with the census being taken, he missed Christmas. And he missed Christ, just like so many people today. With all of the shopping and all of the parties and all of the events, they miss it.

The Religious Leaders Missed Christmas

The religious teachers completely missed Jesus.

Herod called these theological experts in after the wise men asked, "Where is He who has been born King of the Jews?" (Matthew 2:2).

They knew the answer all right. It was Bethlehem. They could quote chapter and verse to the evil king. And yet these men—the supposed guardians of spiritual truth in Israel—wouldn't bother to walk a few miles south to Bethlehem to find out whether the Messiah of Israel had indeed been born.

At least Herod feared Jesus' authority—and tried to nip it in the bud. The innkeeper could claim busyness and ignorance. But what about these men? They knew better. They knew the Word of God, yet they did nothing to respond to it. They were indifferent. They were too busy with themselves to be concerned about Jesus. In fact, when His public ministry began, they became His principal adversaries.

For all practical purposes, these were the very men responsible for the execution of Jesus Christ. Why? Because He was a threat to their little religious empire. The Bible says they sent Jesus up to Pilate out of envy. They envied His authority. They envied the fact that the people loved Him and hung on His every word. They envied the fact that He seemed to have a relationship with God that they lacked.

Addressing this at a later date, Jesus said,

Isaiah was right when he prophesied about you hypocrites; as it is written:

> *"These people honor me with their lips,*
> *but their hearts are far from me.*
> *They worship me in vain;*
> *their teachings are but rules taught by men."*[2]

They were looking for a different kind of a Messiah. They didn't want a Messiah who would suffer and die on a cross for them. They were looking for someone who would support their religious system and their chosen way of living—someone who would cater to their whims and conform to their wishes. Someone who would keep them in power.

There are many people like this today. They want Jesus, but they want Him on their terms.

They want the kind of Jesus they can control, the kind of Jesus who will never challenge them, the kind of Jesus who won't ask them to change their ways.

They want heaven, but they don't want to talk about hell. They want forgiveness, but they are unwilling to repent. They want the cross, but they don't want Christ.

I heard a true story about a woman who went into a jewelry store and began looking at various crosses and crucifixes. After examining them for a while, she said to the jeweler, "Do you have any crosses without this little man on them?"

That's how it is for many people today. They want religion, but only according to their own sensibilities. They want truth, but only if it aligns with "their truth."

The fact is, religion can be a deadly trap. When all is said and done, more people will be sent to hell by religion than by all of the wicked and sinful vices this world has to offer.

The Political Leaders Missed Christmas

King Herod missed Christmas. In fact, he tried to stop it from happening. When the wise men said they were looking for the one who had been born King of the Jews, they couldn't have said a more provocative thing to this paranoid king and puppet of Rome. So he tried to kill Christ. He failed in that effort, of course, but he succeeded in killing untold numbers of baby boys in the process, bringing great sorrow and mourning to Bethlehem. Soon he, too, would be dead and facing his Creator with blood-stained hands.

And then there was the entire empire of Rome. They had established the worldwide census, and Roman soldiers and officials were everywhere, making sure that everyone complied. They had a government and a bureaucracy capable of tracking the taxes of millions of citizens across the known world. But somehow, they missed it when God Himself entered the Roman world and came to visit humanity. Busy with their other gods and the business of ruling an empire, they overlooked the One who would be greater than a thousand empires.

It's a warning to all of us.

It's possible to get a great many things right in life — the right college, the right career, the right city, the right neighborhood — and miss the most important thing of all.

6

DON'T LOSE JESUS

Peple are psycho about getting good deals on certain electronic gift items.

As you may remember, an employee of Wal-Mart in Long Island, New York, was *trampled to death* as the crowd waiting outside the door stampeded into the store to find a little savings. Other workers also were trampled as they tried to rescue the stricken man. At least four people, including a woman who was eight months pregnant, were taken to hospitals. In Tennessee, yet another person was trampled at the entrance of Toys R Us when it opened its doors. Thankfully, this person survived. At another crowded Toys R Us in Palm Desert, California, two men pulled guns and shot each other to death after the women who were with them began to brawl.

Maybe we all should take a deep breath for a moment and

remember what this time is all about.

I've never enjoyed the shopping aspect of Christmas. Not long ago, I heard the story of a couple of men who decided to go sailing instead of Christmas shopping with their wives. So they got out their sailboat, launched it, and were making their way out into the ocean. As it happened, a big December storm slammed into them when they were out to sea, and despite their best efforts, the boat took on a lot of water. As they got close to shore, they were beached on a sandbar. Chest-deep in the freezing water, they tried mightily to free their boat from the sand, but the big waves rolling in kept slamming them up against the side of the hull.

After their third or fourth attempt, one man said to the other, "Sure beats Christmas shopping, doesn't it?"

It seems like we have certainly lost the name of Jesus somewhere in the confusion and chaos of the Christmas celebration. As a matter of fact, you won't even see the word *Christmas* as much as you used to. It has been replaced with the milquetoast "holidays" or "winter solstice."

In much of our country, we have lost sight of the authentic Christmas altogether. In the process, I think we have also lost sight of God.

You Have His Full Attention

Whenever I am out and about with my granddaughter Stella, I have to keep my eye on her at every moment—especially in a toy store. Because if you are with a child in a toy store and you're not holding her hand, she will disappear in the blink of an eye. You will look up at something for what seems like a millisecond, look back, and the child will be gone. She will be darting up and down different aisles, checking everything out. As a result, I always keep my eye on Stella, even though she doesn't necessarily have her eye on me.

In the same way, we sometimes lose sight of God. It is not because He is rushing around or darting in and out of the galaxies; it's because *we* get distracted by or absorbed in so many things. Then, when we finally look up again, it's hard to see Him.

But here's the good news: Even though we lose sight of God, He never loses sight of us. Remember the blessing that the priests in the Old Testament were given to pray over the people? It went like this:

> *The LORD bless you and keep you;*
> *The LORD make His face shine upon you,*
> *And be gracious to you;*
> *The LORD lift up His countenance upon you,*
> *And give you peace. (Numbers 6:24-26)*

It's an incredibly beautiful blessing, and maybe even one that we have read or spoken over others. But have we really understood what it *means*? That phrase, "the Lord lift up His countenance," could be translated "to look, to see, to know, to be interested in, to have one's full attention." Here then, is what God is saying: "I will bless you, I will keep you, and you will have My full attention through the days of your life."

Have you ever been speaking to someone—maybe pouring your heart out to them—and they look distracted? Maybe as soon as you pause for breath, they pull out their smartphone and start checking e-mail. Or they actually take a call while you're in the middle of unburdening your soul. They will say, "Could you hold that thought just for a second? . . . Hello? Hey! What's up? . . . No, I'm not doing anything. . . . Yeah . . . I'll get right back to you."

What you realize in that moment is that your "friend" really isn't all that interested in your life. He pretends to care for a moment or two but really doesn't. He's just looking for a reason to end the conversation and walk away.

Aren't you glad the Lord doesn't take phone calls when you're talking to Him? ("Hello? . . . Gabriel? Listen, I'll get right back to you. I'm in a conversation that I'll wrap up in a second or two.") When you are pouring your heart out to Him, He is taking in every word. Beyond that, He is weighing the emotions and thoughts behind your words. And He knows the thoughts and feelings you can't even express. His eyes aren't glancing around the room, and He isn't checking His watch. He is engaged with you, 100 percent.

When that thought occurred to King David, it staggered him. He wrote these words in one of his psalms: "How precious it is, Lord, to realize that you are thinking about me constantly! I can't even count how many times a day your thoughts turn toward me. And when I waken in the morning, you are still thinking of me!" (Psalm 139:17-18, TLB).

In times of stress or disappointment, you might find yourself wondering whether God is even aware of what might be unfolding in your life. Count on it: He *is* aware. He knows your story and the million stories behind your story.

The essential message of Christmas is that God came to us. He took the initiative. He is always watching you, always caring for you.

You may remember the story from the gospel of Mark, where Jesus dispatched His disciples across the Sea of Galilee while He stayed behind to pray: "When evening came, the boat was in the middle of the lake, and he was alone on land. He saw the disciples straining at the oars, because the wind was against them. About the fourth watch of the night he went out to them, walking on the lake" (Mark 6:47-48, NIV).

They couldn't see Him, but He could see them and He knew their situation. He knew the wind was against them.

He knew they had exhausted themselves, straining at the oars. He knew they were frightened and discouraged. Ultimately, He came to them across the stormy waters.

It's no different with you. He is watching you. He is praying for you. He knows when you feel outmatched, outgunned, and overwhelmed. And He will come to you, straight through your storm, even though you may have lost sight of Him in the night and the swirling clouds.

There was a time in the life of Jesus when Mary and Joseph lost sight of Him for a few days.

Where Is Jesus?

It really happened. Mary and Joseph literally lost Jesus! They misplaced Him—lost Him in the shuffle.

Jesus was twelve years old at the time, and Mary and Joseph had taken Him with them to the temple in Jerusalem for Passover. But somehow, in the busyness of the holiday celebration, they lost track of their Boy. When they got down the road a good distance, they finally realized (to their alarm) that He wasn't with them.

In some ways, it presents a good parallel to the difficulty we have in keeping Jesus in focus at this time of year that is supposed to be about Him. With all the pressures and activities, in all the parties and celebrations and events, we might very well lose sight of the Lord.

My friend Bob Coy, pastor of Calvary Chapel Fort Lauderdale, has a little boy named Christian. One night when he and Christian knelt for prayer by the boy's bedside, Christian prayed, "And, God, thank You for sending Your only forgotten Son."

It was a mistake. He meant to say, "Your only *begotten* Son."

It makes for a cute story, but there's some truth in what the little boy prayed. For many believers, even at Christmas, Jesus Christ has become God's only forgotten Son.

Let me illustrate: Let's say that it is your fortieth birthday, and a large party is being given to celebrate that milestone. All of your friends come to the party, and there are presents in abundance and a huge cake with fancy writing in frosting. Your friends get so into the occasion that they actually go out and record songs about you that repeat your name over and over.

So there it is: A big party and lots of excitement and hoopla. But somehow in all this commotion, no one remembered to invite you, the guest of honor, to your own party!

You assume that it was just an oversight, and you decide to show up at the party anyway, assured that once you arrive, the guests will welcome you with open arms. You arrive at the house, where you see your name emblazoned in lights, and you can hear your name being sung in song after song. But nobody responds to your knock at the door, and the door is locked. The music is so loud they can't hear you, and the people are so busy they don't see you. Finally, you shrug your shoulders, walk away from your own party, and drive home.

This is a picture of Christmas for many of us today. We string our lights, decorate our tree, run around buying gifts for those we love (and more gifts for those we don't love)—all because we feel pressured to do so. We go to countless events and run around like crazy people. But then we have to ask ourselves, has God's only begotten Son become God's only *forgotten* Son? Have we lost God at Christmas? Is that possible?

Yes, it certainly is. And many of us have experienced such a loss, just as Joseph and Mary lost the Boy Jesus in the milling crowds at Passover.

We don't know a lot about the upbringing of Jesus. We know He would have been raised by Joseph, His stepfather or guardian, though he wasn't Jesus' biological father. He would have been taught the craft of carpentry, because Joseph was a carpenter. As a result, Jesus would have been good with His hands.

He certainly would have been a hard worker, and He would have known how to build a table, a chair, a plow, or even a house. I am sure He was a master craftsman. Can you imagine Jesus, the One who created the world, doing shoddy work? I can't. He was what you might describe today as a blue-collar worker. He would go to the synagogue or temple on the Sabbath. He was obedient to His parents.

At the same time, however, there has never been a man who

walked the earth like Jesus, because He was God in human form. He never sinned, never lost His temper, and never did anything wrong at all. While He grew physically in the normal way, He never bounced back and forth between sin and obedience the way that you and I do. No, Jesus went from faith to faith, from grace to grace, from strength to strength, and from obedience to new levels of obedience. But at the same time, Dr. Luke points out that Jesus Christ the Boy (and later the Man) grew up physically, mentally, and spiritually.

This brings up an interesting question. Since Jesus was God, did He have the full knowledge of God when He was that little baby in the manger in Bethlehem? In other words, did He lay there in that little manger of straw and think, *I am the Creator of the universe*?

Did He sit up in the manger and say words like these: "Hello, Mary, Joseph. How are you? Good to see you. Listen, I need a little help getting out of this manger. By the way, could someone change My diaper? I would really appreciate that"?

No. He was God, but He also was an authentic human baby. The almighty Creator of all things, with unlimited strength, had chosen to be dependent on a mother for His nourishment and nurture as any other little baby would.

We know He grew in height and strength and wisdom over a period of time. Luke 2:40 says that "the child grew up healthy and strong. He was filled with wisdom, and God's favor was on him" (NLT). Then in verse 52, we read that "as Jesus continued to grow in body and mind, he grew also in the love of God and of those who knew him" (PH).

Joseph, Mary, and Jesus had traveled to Jerusalem for the annual Passover celebration. After spending several days among the thousands of Jews thronging the capital, they packed up and headed for home. Back in those days, the men traveled after the women. The women would go on ahead, and the men would follow along behind. So Joseph no doubt assumed that young Jesus was traveling with Mary, and Mary assumed that He was with Joseph.

When they had gone a day's journey down the road, however, they discovered, to their shock and dismay, that Jesus was absent. He hadn't been with the women, and He hadn't been with the men. He hadn't been with the cousins or the neighbors. No one had seen Him.

They had forgotten Jesus!

Can you imagine that conversation?

"So where is Jesus?"

"He's with you—isn't He?"

"I don't have Jesus. I thought He was with you."

"I don't have Him, either."

"Where is Jesus? How can we lose Jesus?"

"Where did you see Him last?"

"I saw Him at the temple."

"Well, let's go back there."

This brings up the point that Jesus was ordinary in appearance. He didn't glow in the dark or have a shining halo over His head. If that had been true, He would have been easy to find. Mary and Joseph could have simply said, "Anybody seen a glowing Child? He's the one with the halo and the shiny robe. You can't miss Him."

But no, Jesus didn't glow. It would appear from Scripture that He was as ordinary a man as you could imagine. In fact, when Judas Iscariot went to the Garden of Gethsemane to identify Him to the authorities, he had to say, "He'll be the one I kiss. That's the one you need to arrest."

Jesus didn't stand out from the crowd. In Isaiah 53 we read, "But in our eyes there was no attractiveness at all, nothing to make us want him" (verse 2, TLB).

So in all the hubbub of a huge religious celebration, Mary and Joseph had forgotten the One whom the Passover was all about. They went back and eventually found Him in the temple, "sitting in the midst of the teachers, both listening to them and asking them questions" (Luke 2:46). When Joseph and Mary tried to correct Him, He said, "Did you not know that I must be about My Father's business?" (verse 49).

To me, this story depicts today's Christmas celebrations. We get caught up in all the noise and activities and confusion, and we forget the One we claim to be honoring. He gets left behind somewhere in the crowd.

Don't lose God this Christmas. Don't forget about Jesus in all the parties and celebrations—and even church services. Find those quiet moments in quiet places where you can draw near to Him, speak to Him, and hear His voice.

Losing Him in Our Busyness

Sometimes when we get busy, we start to cut out what we consider to be nonessentials. People will say, "I'm really swamped right now. I don't have time to do everything I normally do. I don't have time to read the Bible. I don't have time to pray."

It always intrigues me when I hear people say things like that. Really? You don't have time to read your Bible? Maybe you should *make* time for that. Maybe there are some things you could cut out so you would have a little bit more time for Bible study. You always will find time for what is important to you, no matter what. And the last thing you ought to cut out is time spent praying and studying the Word, getting you ready for the day. But often that is the first to get tossed out of the daily schedule.

Sometimes we can even get too busy doing good or "spiritual" things. The classic example of this is the story of Mary and Martha, when Jesus came to visit. Jesus liked spending time with the two sisters and their brother, Lazarus. And Martha was probably an excellent cook. Jesus liked to go over to her home. I wonder if He ever just showed up and said, "Hey, Mary and Martha, how's it going? I brought the twelve disciples with Me. Could you make us lunch?"

Martha would say, "Lord, it would be my privilege. You guys sit down. Make yourself comfortable." And they all would wait while she whipped up one of her famous feasts. That was Martha. She showed her love for Jesus in a tangible, practical way.

Mary, who also loved Jesus with all her heart, was a little different from her sister and may have been more "tuned in" spiritually. On one occasion when Jesus showed up, Martha made a beeline for the kitchen and started throwing pots and pans around, planning to prepare a feast fit for a king because, well, He *was* a King.

Mary didn't head for the kitchen with her sister, but planted herself at Jesus' feet, not wanting to miss a single word. Martha, red-faced and perspiring as she chopped up meat and vegetables and started baking bread, glanced out into the living room from time to time to see her sister, paying rapt attention to the Lord, forgetting all else.

It made Martha mad.

Unable to contain her frustration any longer, she burst into the room and interrupted the Lord's words. (Can you imagine?) There was God Almighty, sharing truths of eternity in the living room, and she interrupted to say, in essence, "Excuse me, excuse me. Sorry to bother You, but I could use a little help in the kitchen. Lord, would You tell my sister to get up and start helping me a little?"

I love how Jesus answered His friend: "Martha, dear Martha, you're fussing far too much and getting yourself worked up over nothing. One thing only is essential, and Mary has chosen it — it's the main course, and won't be taken from her" (Luke 10:41-42, MSG).

The fact is, we can become so busy working *for* God that we miss time *with* God. When we think about people who are far from God, we tend to think of those who have left the fellowship of believers, stopped reading their Bibles, and then made a series of really stupid and destructive life decisions. But don't fool yourself. You can be attending church every Sunday, serving on three church committees, and still lose sight of Jesus.

It reminds me of the story of the prodigal sons. (There actually were *two* prodigals in the story Jesus told.) One went out to a far country, wasted all of his money on crazy living, came to his senses, returned home, and was welcomed by the father. The other prodigal son never left home at all. But he was resentful to the core when his brother came back and was given a full pardon, and he let his dad know it. In reality, even though he showed up at the breakfast table every day and punched in on time at work, his heart was miles and miles from the heart of his father.

A prodigal, then, can be outside of the church or inside the church.

In the account in Luke 2, Mary and Joseph lost Jesus and started looking for Him. Where did they finally find Him? Right where they last left Him! He was still there.

It's the same with us. Maybe, if you were honest, you would admit there was a time in your life when you were spiritually stronger and more excited about your faith in Christ than you are today. You might say (with regret), "Well, yes, when I was younger, my fervor for God and my passion for Christ was much greater than it is now. But that was a different time and season. I'll probably never be able to recover that again."

Really? I beg to differ. I think you can recover that lost passion. How? Why not do what Mary and Joseph did? Go back to the last place you were with Him. Go back to that place where you lost Him. He's still there. He is in the same place He always has been, and He is there right now, waiting for you to return. As the old saying goes, "If you feel far from God, guess who moved?"

God hasn't gone anywhere. You are the one who moved off in a different direction and lost sight of Him.

There are some things you never outgrow, never get beyond. Being a Christian isn't rocket science; it's really not that complicated. God has told us there are certain disciplines we must have in our lives if we want to grow spiritually. And one of those is regular Bible study. You don't get past that.

Yet I am amazed there are believers who have known the Lord for years and can't remember the last time they cracked open the Bible and asked God to speak to them. And then they say, "God never talks to me!" Maybe it's because they so rarely open up His Book! God *will* speak to your heart if you open His Word and diligently seek Him.

I know people who have no prayer life to speak of. You don't get beyond that. No believer can honestly say, "Well, I used to pray, but I don't need to anymore." *Yes, you do.* Listen to Paul's commands to the Thessalonians: "Rejoice always, pray without ceasing, in everything give thanks; for this is the will of God in Christ Jesus for you" (1 Thessalonians 5:16-18). You say, "How does that work? I'd never get anything done if I spent all day and all night on my knees."

That is not what Paul is talking about. What he is saying is to live your life in an attitude of prayer. Keep the contact open. Shoot up prayers to Him on the details of your day, and be listening for His voice as He speaks to your heart.

Have you ever been talking to someone on their cell phone, and they neglected to end the call? You can hear them talking and walking around, but they have no idea they are still connected to you and that the line is open. This verse is saying to do this deliberately with God. Don't hang up on Him. Keep that call going all day and all night. (And by the way, you will never run out of minutes. God always picks up the bill for that.)

And then there are those Christians who aren't in fellowship with God's people at all. Where did Mary and Joseph find Jesus? They found Him in the house of God. Where are you going to find Jesus? In the same place! I'm not talking about a particular building. The house of God is wherever God's people are gathered together — for worship, for Bible study, for fellowship, for service, and all the rest. If you aren't plugged in to a local fellowship where people know your face and your name, it will result in your spiritual downfall.

The Bible says, "Let us not neglect our meeting together, as some people do, but encourage one other, especially now that the day of his return is drawing near" (Hebrews 10:25, NLT).

How clear is that? Christ could not only return in our lifetime, but He could return this year — or tomorrow. So when He comes, let Him find you with God's people, worshiping, growing, and encouraging one another.

Have you lost sight of Jesus in this season of your life? Have you overlooked Him in this hectic, sometimes pressured Christmas season? Maybe you have simply forgotten about Him as the years have passed by. I have good news for you. God has not forgotten about you.

You will find Him right where you left Him.

He is there for you at this very moment.

Do you hear His voice?

He says, "Be still, and know that I am God."[1]

WHAT THE WISE MEN UNDERSTOOD

We know the Christmas card image so well.

There are always three of them, wearing turbans, riding on camels, and silhouetted against a night sky. A huge, magnificent star blazes on the horizon. Tradition has given them names: Gaspar, Melchior, and Balthasar. They even have their own song to sing (in three-part harmony) as they plod along through the sandy wastes, seeking a newborn King:

> *We three kings of Orient are*
> *Bearing gifts we traverse afar*
> *Field and fountain, moor and mountain*
> *Following yonder star*

The Bible, however, never says there were only three, doesn't mention camels, and doesn't give them names.

Let's peel this tradition back and find out who these mysterious men from the East really were and what they have to teach us about worship.

The Bible calls them Magi. We get our English words *magic* and *magician* from this same term. These were men who consulted the stars and were experts in both astronomy and astrology. Rulers, kings, and pharaohs sought out their counsel and guidance. In contrast to the seers, prophets, and priests of Scripture, the Magi used sorcery, wizardry, and witchcraft, combining science and mathematics with delvings into the occult. Over the years, their religious and political influence continued to grow until they became the most prominent and powerful group of advisors in the Medo-Persian and Babylonian empires.

These Magi, then, steeped in occultism and false religion, became very powerful and were almost like royalty themselves. They wouldn't have worn the pajama-and-bathrobe kind of outfits (with the pointy shoes) that we see depicted on Christmas cards; they would have dressed in a way befitting their status and high office. And they wouldn't have ridden camels; they probably entered Jerusalem astride magnificent Arabian stallions. Most likely, they had a small army riding with them for protection. No wonder they created such a stir when that whole resplendent cavalcade rode through the gates of Jerusalem! It was like a foreign army coming in. Most likely, no one had ever seen anything like it.

To top it off, the question they immediately started asking must have swept through the streets like a stiff wind: *Where is He who is born king of the Jews?* In no time at all, the question went viral!

And here is one more blow to our cherished story: The wise men were not present at the manger in Bethlehem on the night Jesus was born. Shepherds, yes. Wise men, no. The Bible says in Matthew 2:11, "When [the wise men] had come into the house" (not the manger), "they saw the young Child" (not the Baby) "with Mary His mother, and fell down and worshiped Him."

Nevertheless, these wise men from the East knew something that Herod and most others would never know: This little Toddler in a tiny, humble house, born to common working-class people, would one day rule the world.

The Magi brought Him gifts befitting a king: gold, frankincense, and myrrh. (Just a little note here about these gifts: You can safely bet they weren't wrapped in paper. Why do I say that? Because of two important characteristics about those who gave the gifts. First, they were wise; and second, they were *men*. Men hate wrapping gifts.)

These Magi, pagan though they may have been, understood something right off the bat that many people today never understand.

They understood that Christmas is about worship.

The religious leaders in Jerusalem knew the Scriptures well enough to point the Magi in the right direction in their search for this newborn king.

When Herod the king heard this, he was troubled, and all Jerusalem with him. And when he had gathered all the chief priests and scribes of the people together, he inquired of them where the Christ was to be born.

So they said to him, "In Bethlehem of Judea, for thus it is written by the prophet:

'But you, Bethlehem, in the land of Judah,
Are not the least among the rulers of Judah;
For out of you shall come a Ruler
Who will shepherd My people Israel.'" (Matthew 2:3-6)

Now they had a specific direction: Bethlehem, less than twenty miles away. But how would they find the one particular Child among all the children of that town and region?

God sent the star ahead of them.

When they heard the king, they departed; and behold, the star which they had seen in the East went before them, till it came and stood over where the young Child was. When they saw the star, they rejoiced with exceedingly great joy. And when they had come into the house, they saw the young Child with Mary His mother, and fell down and worshiped Him. And when they had opened their treasures, they presented gifts to Him: gold, frankincense, and myrrh. (verses 9–11)

When they received that specific direction from God, they were overcome with joy. Picture your most joyful moment in life, and then multiply it by ten. These men had traveled vast distances through desolate and dangerous lands over many weeks, and now they were receiving strong confirmation that they were right on track and right on schedule. They were going to be granted the privilege of seeing a king whose destiny had been written in the stars.

What did they do when they finally found the house and the young Child? They fell down and worshiped Him.

Let me ask you a question: What would make this a perfect Christmas for you? Maybe you're thinking, *If I could just get this one thing I've really been hoping for. . . . I left a detailed map for my parents so they could find the store. . . . I sent an e-mail with a link so that my wife could order it online. . . . I left a written hint in my husband's briefcase.*

Or maybe it would be a perfect Christmas for you if your loved one really enjoys your gift, the one you have been scheming about and planning for almost a year. If he or she is truly surprised or touched or excited or blown away . . . ah, that would just make the day for you.

The trouble is, the events of life hardly ever live up to our expectations. And Christmas is usually loaded with all kinds of expectations. We hope the relationship with the in-laws will go better. We hope the dinner will come together the way we planned it. We hope everyone will get along. We hope that our hearts will be overflowing with emotions of nostalgia or peace or happiness.

Maybe these things will happen, and maybe they won't. But placing our hopes and desires on events turning out a certain way is usually a recipe for a big letdown.

The wise men, however, were particularly wise in the way they celebrated the birth of the King. They worshiped Him. But it wasn't just saying "Merry Christmas" to people on the street or humming "We Three Kings" when they got up in the morning. The Bible says they fell down and worshiped Him. In other words, they gave themselves completely to praising and adoring the young King.

Another translation of Matthew 2:11 reads like this: "They entered the house and saw the child in the arms of Mary, his mother. Overcome, they kneeled and worshiped him" (MSG).

Immediately afterward, they opened their treasure bags and presented the Child with their precious gifts. Soon after this, God warned them in a dream not to go back through Jerusalem, but to go home a different way. So they were still receiving direction from on high! God was still directing their path.

I have a question for you: Do you think these men went home disappointed? Do you think they left Bethlehem feeling deflated or let down or depressed? Far from it! I think this must have been the crowning event of their whole lives. Through all their years, they would talk about the star, the young King, and the opportunity they had been given to worship Him with all their hearts and offer Him gifts.

This is one activity that will never disappoint. Wholehearted worship of Jesus Christ, giving Him your best, giving Him yourself, always will fill your soul rather than deplete it.

The truth is, however, everyone worships at Christmas.

They may be politically correct and not even utter the word *Christmas*. They may not have a Nativity scene or an inflated Santa Claus on their front lawn. It doesn't matter. Skeptics worship. Humbugs worship. Atheists and agnostics worship. Radical environmentalists, feminists, and mainstream media personalities worship. Conservative Republicans and liberal Democrats and confirmed Independents worship. Even lawyers worship.

You say, "Greg, I beg to differ with you. Some of those people you mentioned don't worship at all."

I didn't say they worship *God*. I said they worship. Everyone bows at the altar of something. They may not call it a deity, but it is something they are committed to and passionate about. It is something they believe in. Some people bow at the altar of material things. They worship their possessions: a car, a house, a boat, a bank account. These are their gods.

Other people worship their own bodies. They've never met a mirror they didn't love. They spend hours studying exotic diets or sculpting their bodies at the gym or injecting strange things into their face to remove wrinkles. Their own physical appearance is their god.

Other people worship a god of their own making. They say things like, "Well, *my* god never would judge a person for doing something wrong. *My* god is all-loving and all-caring and all-tolerant." But what god is that? In effect, they have created a god in their own image and according to their own notions of right and wrong.

But here is the problem: You can bow at these altars, but none of these gods is able to save you. None of these gods is going to help you. And quite frankly, none of these gods is worthy of your worship. There is only one God who is worthy of your worship — the living Triune God, Father, Son, and Holy Spirit.

How, then, do we do it? How do we worship the Lord?

One way is by singing, perhaps some of the great carols of the season. That is one of the things I love about the Christian faith: We have all the killer songs! Why is that? Because we have something worth singing about. There is victory and joy and hope and celebration and honor in the songs we sing. What's more, all our singing here is just a warm-up act for eternity.

Take a moment to contemplate the awesome scene described in Revelation 5:

Then I looked, and I heard the voice of many angels around the throne, the living creatures, and the elders; and the number of them was ten thousand times ten thousand, and thousands of thousands, saying with a loud voice:

> *"Worthy is the Lamb who was slain*
> *To receive power and riches and wisdom,*
> *And strength and honor and glory and blessing!"*

And every creature which is in heaven and on the earth and under the earth and such as are in the sea, and all that are in them, I heard saying:

> *"Blessing and honor and glory and power*
> *Be to Him who sits on the throne,*
> *And to the Lamb, forever and ever!"*

Then the four living creatures said, "Amen!" And the twenty-four elders fell down and worshiped Him who lives forever and ever. (verses 11–14)

The elders fell down and worshiped the Lord, just as the wise men did at the little house in Bethlehem. And as you and I worship Him with all our hearts, we can enter into joy that will never, ever fade.

However, we don't always feel like praising the Lord. In fact, if the truth were known, it is sometimes the *last* thing we feel like doing. Yet that is the very time when our praise and thanksgiving mean the most. Hebrews 13:15 tells us, "Through Jesus, therefore, let us continually offer to God a sacrifice of praise—the fruit of lips that confess his name" (NIV).

When we praise God even when we don't feel like it, when we praise God through our disappointment or sorrow or tears, we are offering a sacrifice that pleases Him. Think what it means to you when someone you care about gives you a gift or card, looks you in the eyes, and says, "I love you." That expression, if you know it's really from the heart, means more than the gift, doesn't it? In the same way, the Lord likes it when we say to Him, "Lord, I love You," and express that in our worship and praise.

But that is not the only way that we can show our praise to God and offer our worship to the Lord. Another way that we worship God is through serving others. One of the ways the word *worship* is translated in the Bible is "to serve and minister."

We looked at Hebrews 13:15, which speaks about the sacrifice of praise. But the very next verse goes on like this: "And do not forget to do good and to share with others, for with such sacrifices God is pleased" (verse 16, NIV).

A popular paraphrase of that same verse says,

> *Make sure you don't take things for granted and go slack in work-ing for the common good; share what you have with others. God takes particular pleasure in acts of worship —a different kind of "sacrifice"—that take place in kitchen and workplace and on the streets.* (MSG)

Most of us think of worship as what we do when we sing songs and hymns, close our eyes, and lift our hands. And indeed, that can be worship. But worship can also be that meal you cook for a sick friend or that clothing or financial help you provide for someone in need.

I remember when I was in Billy and Ruth Graham's home in North Carolina years ago before she went to heaven. Ruth had placed a sign over her kitchen sink that read "Divine service is conducted here three times a day." It's true. Even washing dishes for your family or friends can be an act of worship.

Bringing Our Gifts to Him

Another way we can worship is through our giving to the Lord. In Matthew 2:11, we read that when the Magi "had opened their treasures, they presented gifts to Him: gold, frankincense, and myrrh."

When you get a gift for someone, you start thinking about it ahead of time, don't you? If you really care about that person, you put some thought and care into finding just the right gift. You reflect on what you know about that individual and try to come up with something that will be a good "fit" and represent your love for the person. You search for that gift. You set money aside and save for it. And then you go out and find it and bring it home.

When we think of the gift of Jesus—His coming to earth to die for our sins—it wasn't an afterthought with God or an "impulse." The Bible says that Jesus was "slain from the foundation of the world" (Revelation 13:8). What does that mean? It means that long before there was a little town of Bethlehem or a garden called Eden or even a planet called Earth, a decision was made in the councils of eternity that God would come to the earth as a man to redeem His creation.

Why? Because God knew that man would blow it. God knew that Adam and Eve would eat of the forbidden fruit. The Lord knew that we would sin, and that if He was to have a relationship with His fallen creation, there would have to be atonement. A sacrifice had to be made. It was all part of God's plan from the very beginning. That is how much thought He put into the gift He gave to each of us, the gift of eternal life.

I don't understand people who go to someone's birthday party without some kind of present in hand. It has always seemed to me that if I am invited to a party for someone, I am there to celebrate that person and I ought to bring something. It doesn't have to be expensive or a big deal. It might just be a handmade card. It might be a cappuccino from Starbucks. I just don't want to walk through the door of my friend's house empty-handed on the day that he or she is being honored.

Everyone knows that Christmas is the Lord Jesus' birthday party. Should we enter the celebration empty-handed? What do we give to God? What does He really want?

Answer: He wants you.

That is the gift you can give to the Lord as you celebrate His birth. You can give yourself.

Paul said in Romans 12:1, "I urge you, brothers, in view of God's mercy, to offer your bodies as living sacrifices, holy and pleasing to God—this is your spiritual act of worship" (NIV). Another translation of that same verse says,

> So here's what I want you to do, God helping you: Take your everyday, ordinary life—your sleeping, eating, going-to-work, and walking-around life—and place it before God as an offering. Embracing what God does for you is the best thing you can do for him. (MSG)

Bring your life to God.
Bring your time to God.
Bring your health to God.
Bring your family to God.

Bring your worries and concerns to God.

Bring your future to God.

Say, "Lord, this is what I offer to You."

Why do I do this? Because God is good, and He is worthy of my praise. The Bible says, "Oh, give thanks to the LORD, for He is good! For His mercy endures forever" (Psalm 107:1). That verse doesn't say, "Give thanks to the Lord, because you've had a good year" or "Give thanks to the Lord, because everything is going so well in your life."

The truth is, events in our lives don't always go well. As residents of a broken planet, we experience pain, disappointments, setbacks, and sorrow. But God is still good and worthy of our praise.

What are you worshiping? If you are bowing at the altar of Christmas this year, you will be deeply disappointed because Christmas — the holiday — cannot deliver on its promises. It can never, ever live up to all the hype. It can't bring you inner peace, much less peace on earth. It can't bring you the joy and fulfillment you crave. Christmas always will let you down.

What is Christmas at its worst? It is a crass, commercial, empty, exhausting, and very expensive ritual that drags on endlessly for months. And then bills come due. What is Christmas at its best? It is a promise of things to come — a glimpse of what still lies in our future. The beauty . . . the worshipful music . . . the adoring angels . . . the love . . . the warmth . . . the security . . .

the nearness of God . . . the promise . . . the gathering of friends and family . . . it is all promised to us in a life to come. Yes, we get a glimpse of it now, but more is coming later.

What we need this year is not "the promise of Christmas." That is a promise filled with holes and disappointment. What we need is the promise of Christ. We need the Messiah, not merriment. We need God, not goodwill. We need His presence, not just presents. We need the living, radiant, all-powerful, resurrected Jesus Christ, not a figurine in a manger scene.

Anything or anyone else will fall short of this.

If you worship a god of your own making, he or she or it will disappoint you. But if you worship the true and living God, He never will disappoint you — not now, not in a trillion years.

Here is the thing we often overlook when we think about the birth of Jesus: The beautiful Child born in the manger in Bethlehem was born to die. It is hard for us to think about the fact that those soft baby hands one day would grow into the hands of a strong Man and have spikes driven through them. It's difficult for us to consider the fact that those little feet of the Baby Jesus one day would be nailed to a cross of wood. It is painful to remember that the soft little forehead of the Baby Jesus in the manger, so loved by His mother, one day would be crowned with thorns.

This Child came with a purpose. From the moment He stepped foot on this earth, Jesus Christ lived in the shadow of the cross. He was born to die that we might live.

Those wise men had it right when they brought the unusual gifts of gold, frankincense, and myrrh. What kind of gifts are those for a kid? But they had an insight into why He came. They gave Him gold, because that Child would one day reign as King. They gave Him frankincense, because they recognized that He would become a High Priest, representing people to God. And they brought Him myrrh, which was the most bizarre gift of all. Myrrh was used for embalming. Why would you bring something so morbid, so inappropriate to a young Child? Because they recognized that this King, this High Priest, would die for our sins.

And He would give us the ultimate gift: His very life.

WHAT THE SHEPHERDS FOUND

Now there were in the same country shepherds living out in the fields, keeping watch over their flock by night. And behold, an angel of the Lord stood before them, and the glory of the Lord shone around them, and they were greatly afraid. Then the angel said to them, "Do not be afraid, for behold, I bring you good tidings of great joy which will be to all people. For there is born to you this day in the city of David a Savior, who is Christ the Lord. And this will be the sign to you: You will find a Babe wrapped in swaddling cloths, lying in a manger."

And suddenly there was with the angel a multitude of the heavenly host praising God and saying:

"Glory to God in the highest,
And on earth peace, goodwill toward men!"

> *So it was, when the angels had gone away from them into heaven, that the shepherds said to one another, "Let us now go to Bethlehem and see this thing that has come to pass, which the Lord has made known to us." And they came with haste and found Mary and Joseph, and the Babe lying in a manger. Now when they had seen Him, they made widely known the saying which was told them concerning this Child. And all those who heard it marveled at those things which were told them by the shepherds. But Mary kept all these things and pondered them in her heart. Then the shepherds returned, glorifying and praising God for all the things that they had heard and seen, as it was told them. (Luke 2:8-20)*

The wise men, as we have noted, weren't around on the night when Jesus was born in that stable in Bethlehem. Most likely, they were still back in their observatories in the mysterious East, studying their charts—and perhaps puzzling over the emergence of a strange new star.

The shepherds, however, were eyewitnesses of the events that night—undoubtedly the most remarkable night in history—when the Son of God was born to a human mother as a tiny Baby.

As a group, the shepherds couldn't have been more different from the Magi. Where the wise men were at the top of the economic scale, the shepherds were at the bottom. In fact, these men were the lowest of the low in the Jewish culture.

Shepherds were despised and mistrusted by the rest of society.

They were thought to be crafty and dishonest, and they weren't allowed to observe the ceremonial hand washings of that day. The testimony of a shepherd wasn't even allowed in a court of law at that time. As men of the field, they smelled just like their work: sheep. The only people lower on the social ladder in Israel were those with leprosy.

Think of all the people to whom God might have brought this stunning message. The angels might have easily appeared in the court of Caesar himself. They could have burst into the court of King Herod with their glad tidings. They could have given the announcement to any number of political, military, or economic leaders of the day.

But God didn't send them to the rich, powerful, or influential.

It was as though He had said, "Who is the lowest of the low? Who are the ones no one cares about? The shepherds—those are the ones to whom I will bring My message." *There is born to you this day in the city of David a Savior, who is Christ the Lord.*

The Lord came to the shepherds where they were, and He came to the Magi where they were.

So what do we learn from this?

God Comes to Us Wherever We Are

Both the shepherds and the wise man received the announcement of Christ's birth. For the shepherds, it came with a stunning display in the heavens and a vast choir of angels declaring the glorious event. For the wise men, it began with the appearance of a mysterious star in the heavens that led them on a long journey to Bethlehem.

A number of years ago, Robert McIvor wrote a book titled *Star of Bethlehem, Star of Messiah*. In this book, he cites records from ancient Chinese and Korean astronomers who recorded an unusual star appearing around the time of Christ's birth. In fact, according to the author, the appearance of a mysterious star was a worldwide event. Some scholars think the star may have been an appearance of the Shechinah glory of God.

Whatever the case, two revelations came to two groups of people, and they both believed God's Word.

At this point in history, there had been four hundred years of silence since the last biblical prophet had spoken. There had been no prophetic utterances, no angelic appearances, and no miracles performed.

And then, heaven broke that silence. God Himself stepped back into human history with angelic appearances to Zechariah, father of John the Baptist; to Mary, the mother of Jesus; and to Joseph, Mary's husband-to-be. Out in the distant East, He began directing the attention of the Magi to a mysterious sight in the heavens. And finally, on the night of Jesus' birth, the night sky was suddenly torn open, with angels unleashing a torrent of praise on a group of frightened shepherds.

The point is that God will come to you wherever you are. No one is beyond His reach.

The shepherds probably were raised in good Jewish homes where they learned about the God of Israel, the God of Abraham, Isaac, and Jacob. The very sheep they were raising may have been intended for temple sacrifices. If that were the case, they would have been very familiar with the need for animal sacrifice in the approach of God under the old covenant.

You might have been raised in a Christian home, having had the privilege of hearing the Word of God since you were a little boy or a little girl. You have heard the name of Jesus as far back as you can remember.

But here is the problem: Sometimes a person who has grown up around Christianity all his or her life can become more spiritually indifferent than a person who has not been. You might be like some of the religious leaders in Israel at that time and know a great many things in your head but have no real relationship with God. You have heard the gospel so many times, and you say, "Yes, yes, I know all that. I've heard that. I don't want to talk about that." Don't let that happen to you. Don't let your heart get hardened toward God.

The wise men, on the other hand, were steeped in superstition, occultism, and false belief. God in no way condoned their pagan lifestyle, but He used a star to reach them, draw them, touch their hearts, and bring them to Himself. Wherever you are, God will reach you.

As I've mentioned, I wasn't raised in a Christian home, had never heard the Bible, and never went to church. But God invaded my world, and I responded to Him. He can invade yours as well. Anyone who is truly seeking Him will find Him. In Jeremiah 29:13, the Lord says, "You will seek Me and find Me, when you search for Me with all your heart." If someone is deceived by a cult or a false belief—as the wise men were—I believe that if they really hunger to know God, He will reveal Himself to them.

That is the story of the whole Bible. It is a record of God's revealing Himself to mankind. He is not a God who hides Himself; He wants men and women to know Him and draw near to Him. In the first chapters of Genesis, what we see is man hiding from God after he had sinned, not God hiding from man. In fact, God came looking for Adam and Eve, calling out, "Where are you?"

In the case of the Magi, God directed followers of the stars through a star that led them to Christ. In other words, He came to where they were to bring them to where they needed to be.

In the same way, as Christians we need to go to where people are with the gospel. Jesus didn't say that the whole world should go to church, but He did say that the church should go to the whole world. We need to be like one of those stars that would bring others to Christ. God can use you in that way.

Many follow the latest antics of Hollywood celebrities. What are they up to now? What party are they going to? Who is dating whom, and who is wearing what? God has zero interest in that. He sees a different kind of star. The person who is a star in God's eyes is the man or woman who will seek to bring others to faith. In fact, we are told over in the book of Daniel, "Men and women who have lived wisely and well will shine brilliantly, like the cloudless, star-strewn night skies. And those who put others on the right path to life will glow like stars forever" (12:3, MSG).

The shepherds and the wise men also worshiped the Lord. Those wise men would not let anything keep them away. Wild horses could not keep them away. The New King James version says, "They came with haste" (Luke 2:16). Another translation says they came running. They were sprinting. They wanted to see for themselves.

I am amazed at what will keep some people away from church: a drop of rain, a sniffle, waking up in a bad mood. People will say, "You know, I just don't feel like going to church today. I'm staying home." But look at what people will endure to go to a football game. I was watching a game on TV the other day where they were playing in a virtual blizzard. A guy would catch a pass and slide for ten yards. And the stands were full! There wasn't an empty seat, even in the snow and windchill. When they did close-ups of the fans in the stadium, they were screaming, yelling, jumping around, and had their faces painted with the team colors.

Yet people will say, "I can't go to church today. It just isn't convenient." And if they do come, and they lift their hands higher than their shoulders during worship, someone close to them will mutter, "Fanatic! That's embarrassing."

If only we would have as much passion for the Lord as some people have for their favorite athletic teams. We believers should have much more passion. What's a national championship? What's the Final Four? What's the World Series? What's the Superbowl? We have been given eternal salvation by our Lord and Savior, and we have the privilege of walking with Him and serving Him through all the days of our lives until He takes us home. Now *that* is something to get excited about!

The Messiah has come. And His name is called Immanuel, *which means God with us.*

It doesn't get any better than that.

We Must Respond to the Call

God came to the wise men and the shepherds at different times and in different ways. But both groups of men had something in common. They *responded* to the call of God. The Magi, in their comfortable dwellings in the distant East, might have said, "Jerusalem? Are you kidding me? Do you know how far away that is? That could take weeks. And then when we get there, who knows what we'll find?"

It wasn't a matter of booking a flight or printing out a map on MapQuest and jumping into their SUV. No, this was a very long journey on horseback or by camel, with all sorts of hazards and trials on the way. But they came. They wanted to see for themselves. Even though they were potentially sacrificing their own prestige and reputation to go to this unknown land, they made that trip, saying, "Where is He who has been born King of the Jews? For we have . . . come to worship Him" (Matthew 2:2).

The shepherds might have stayed away, too. For them, it wasn't such a long journey, but they may very well have felt unworthy and unwanted. Most people didn't like shepherds or want them around. What if they were rejected or turned away?

Have you ever gone someplace where you suddenly felt people weren't glad to see you? You show up at the door, and people look up, then look away. The conversation stops, and the atmosphere suddenly feels awkward or uncomfortable. What a terrible feeling that is. And these shepherds, after all the rejection they had experienced through the years, might have said to each other, "Aw, what's the use? We're not dressed right. We don't know the right things to say. We don't know the protocol. Besides, they won't want us there. Nobody wants shepherds around. We're just one step above people with leprosy."

The Bible says, "They came with haste and found Mary and Joseph, and the Babe lying in a manger" (Luke 2:16). Another translation says they "hurried to the village." They would have been out of breath when they arrived, with their hearts pounding.

They answered God's call quickly.

They Both Believed and Worshiped

Both the Magi and the shepherds made a diligent search for Jesus. When the shepherds left the stable, they "went back to their flocks, glorifying and praising God for all they had heard and seen. It was just as the angel had told them" (Luke 2:20, NLT).

And as we noted earlier, the Magi actually fell down in the presence of the Infant Christ and worshiped Him.

What is seen here is an eagerness to worship Christ. You will hear many people talk about how Christmas has been ruined by crass commercialism or political correctness or all the materialism and buying frenzy associated with it. We might even find ourselves saying we dread the whole holiday.

While it's true that we can't do much about what Christmas has become in our culture, we can look at it through a different set of lenses. We can use it as motivation to worship our Lord. We can emulate the eagerness of the shepherds to be in His presence. We can follow the example of the Magi, who set their hearts to find Him and wouldn't be satisfied with anything less.

We can use this season of the year to thank Jesus for coming, to praise Him for being born on this earth so that He could grow up and die for our sins, opening the door to heaven for us and giving us a reason and purpose for living.

It's interesting to note that we are never commanded in Scripture to remember the birth of Jesus. Of course, there is nothing wrong with doing that; it is a good and worthy thing to do. But we are commanded in Scripture to remember His death. In that Upper Room with His disciples before He went to the cross, Jesus said, "Take, eat; this is My body which is broken for you; do this in remembrance of Me" (1 Corinthians 11:24).

He wants us to remember Him. He wants us to worship Him.

9

THE PROMISE OF CHRISTMAS

I don't know about you, but I have always believed in the promise of Christmas.

There is something very special, wonderful, even magical (in the best sense of that word) about this time of the year. My memories of Christmas go back to my earliest childhood and have grown through the years.

To this day, I feel a sense of wonder, beauty, and anticipation as Christmas approaches. I probably love the same things that you do: being with loved ones, eating incredible food, and watching for the excitement on a small child's face as he or she opens a gift.

It is also a time that, for the most part, is marked by an absence of meanness. Yes, I know the stories of crazed people charging into stores and fighting over the latest electronic devices, and I have seen people almost go to war over parking places at the mall. But often, people will show an extra measure of kindness at this time of year. You might find yourself talking to a person you wouldn't normally talk to. Why? Because it's Christmas, and you suddenly have a few things in common.

You might say "Merry Christmas" to a complete stranger on the street and get the same greeting back—or at least a weak "Happy Holidays."

But here is the question: For all our anticipation of Christmas every year, does it really deliver on its promises?

Yes, sometimes—a little here and a little there. But for the most part, the holiday itself really doesn't deliver on all the hype and hoopla that surrounds it. What it does deliver is a lot of difficulty. If you are a man, your blood pressure will go up dramatically during this time of the year.

I read a newspaper article by a British psychologist who found that shopping is actually hazardous for men's health. The article said that male volunteers from ages twenty-two to seventy-nine were tested by sending them out Christmas shopping. The researchers recorded that the blood pressure of these volunteers shot up to levels that you would see "in a fighter pilot going into combat." When they did the same test on women, however, there was no change in their blood pressure at all. So I guess ladies are just more suited for this kind of stress than we guys are.

Christmas Longings

Ever since I was a little boy, I always wanted a *real* family Christmas. I would watch those programs on TV where the families would gather around the table and carve the turkey and give out the presents. But I never had a stable family growing up, with my mom being married and divorced all those times.

I remember one Christmas in particular where we were sitting around the tree. My mom was passed out from drinking too much. I recall looking at this fake, little white tree with one of those turning wheels and multicolored panes that continually changed the color of the tree. There was Christmas music playing in the background, but the smell of stale smoke and alcohol pervaded the room. Even as a little boy, I thought to myself, *It has got to get better than this.*

And it did!

It began when I was in high school, with receiving Jesus Christ as my Lord and Savior and stepping into a whole new life. But even before I became a Christian, I had determined that I would find the right woman, get married, *stay* married, and give my family a stable, loving home. I didn't want anyone to have to experience what I had experienced growing up in an unhappy, alcoholic home.

I also determined that when I had children, they would have a merry Christmas. God gave Cathe and I two boys, and I can tell you, it is the easiest thing in the world to buy toys for boys when you're a dad. It never was a challenge! I would see something and say, "Hey, this is cool. They will like it." And most of the time, I was right. Now I have granddaughters, and I'm starting at square one. Buying for girls is a completely different experience.

Each year with my boys, I tried to top myself from the Christmas before, probably spending too much money and getting them elaborate gifts. I definitely was more excited than they were on Christmas mornings, wanting them to get up at the first light of dawn with me to see what I had given them. Most of the time, they just wanted to sleep a little longer and open the presents at their leisure.

Then came 2008, the first Christmas after losing Christopher, my thirty-three-year-old son who died in a traffic accident in July of that year. Anyone who has lost a loved one will know what I mean when I say that the Christmas season is laced with emotional landmines. Memories can be triggered by a thousand different things: a song, a scent, a conversation, even someone's casual remark. A recollection seemingly pops up out of nowhere, and you are hit by a wave of pain.

Canceling Christmas?

After considering all of these things for a number of years, I have made a somewhat radical decision. I think we ought to cancel Christmas and make it official right now.

No . . . wait a minute. I guess I don't mean Christmas itself. I love Christmas. But I want to cancel what Christmas has *become* in our culture. I want to cancel this contemporary, generic version of "the holidays" that so many people buy into today.

Or, at the very least, cancel it for myself.

I'm not saying you have to unstring your lights or pitch out your Christmas tree or stop giving presents to each other. (I do, however, think I can make a pretty good case for removing fruitcake from the planet.)

What I am suggesting is that we cancel the hijacked version of Christmas. I think the very word *Christmas* has been pirated, emptied of its meaning, drained of its wonder, cheapened in its value, dragged through the gutter, and given back to us, minus its beauty and power. Let's cancel the version of Christmas that is filled with hype and endless activity, leading to exhaustion and little to any thought of Christ. Let's cancel the Christmas where people bow to political correctness and take anything to do with Jesus right out of the picture. Let's cancel this artificial, counterfeit, commercial holiday we call Christmas or "the holidays" and instead celebrate the birth of Jesus Christ.

I still believe in the promise of Christmas. Not in this holiday as we celebrate it for the most part, but in the real message of Christmas—which is the birth of our Lord and the entrance of our God into time and space and a human body.

Because of our nation's faltering economy, I think many are

bracing themselves for a tough Christmas. Because people aren't able to spend what they used to spend and do all they used to do, they tell themselves (with a sigh) that it won't be Christmas "like it used to be."

No, it may not be like it used to be. And that may be the best news yet. In fact, it may be better—much better.

What if it was a brighter, more peaceful Christmas than any you have experienced before, because you were freed from the pressure of getting stuff from people and people getting stuff from you, because you said, "Let's just forget about all that and be together and think about what all this really means."

That could be a really good Christmas. It actually could be the best Christmas of your life. Why? Because the primary message of Christmas is not "Let it snow" or "Let's shop till we drop." The real message is "Let us worship." That is what the wise men came to do. They said, "Where is He who has been born King of the Jews? For we have seen His star in the East and have come to worship Him" (Matthew 2:2). And when they saw that star leading toward Bethlehem, Scripture says they "rejoiced with exceedingly great joy" (verse 10). The word *exceedingly* means "to the highest measure." The word *great* in the original language is *megas,* from which we get our word *mega*, or gigantic.

So let me do my own translation here: When the wise men knew for sure that God was directing them to Bethlehem where they would see the young King, they were megajoyful, with a happiness that went beyond all measure. I think we can confidently say these men had never been so joyful and excited in their entire lives.

They weren't going to see a Christmas light display or listen to a Christmas concert or attend a Christmas drama, and they didn't have front-row tickets to some big Hollywood-Vegas-style extravaganza.

They were on their way to a simple little house in a tiny little village to see a little toddler, who happened to be the King of kings.

It was the prospect of worship that sent their hearts soaring.

How long has it been since your heart soared like that? How long has it been since you have experienced sheer, beyond-measure, over-the-top joy? Was it when you got a new iPhone? Probably not. Was it when your team scored a touchdown in a big bowl game? How long did that last?

It is worship that brings us deep-down, lasting joy. And no wonder. We were made to worship. It is in our DNA. It is part of our wiring.

Worship releases us from boredom.

Worship lifts our anxieties.

Worship melts away our fears.

Worship restores the sense of wonder we had as children.

That doesn't mean that all our circumstances will be perfect or that our lives will be a stroll through fields of daisies. Not at all. Every one of us will face hardships, challenges, even tragedy. The Bible never teaches that we will have a problem-free, pain-free, or sorrow-free life as a follower of Christ. But the Bible does teach that we never will be alone. And because of that, we don't have to be afraid.

In Psalm 91, the Lord says to the believer, "I will be with him in trouble" (verse 15). Did you catch that? He doesn't say He will shield us *from* trouble, He says that He will be with us *in* trouble.

He will be *with us* in trouble. God will be with us. That is the whole meaning of the word *Immanuel*. And that is the very message our weary, cynical, sin-sick world needs to hear.

If Christmas doesn't "deliver" for you, it is not really the fault of Christmas. It is our fault. We have built up this holiday so much in our minds that no single event could ever really achieve what we are anticipating.

Christmas can't bring harmony to your home.

Christmas can't bring peace on earth.

Christmas can't repair broken or strained relationships.

Christmas can't wash away your sins and regrets.

Christmas can't restore joy to a bitter, unhappy heart.

Christmas can't make you like a little child again.

That is the bad news. But the good news is that Christ Himself—the living Son of God—can do all of this and more. In fact, He can do anything. A holiday can never transform our lives, but Jesus both can and will. And that is what we are really longing for deep inside.

There really is a promise of Christmas, but it is only operative as the promise of Christ Himself.

Anything short of Christ ultimately will disappoint, but He never will.

A few years ago, I blogged about how difficult Christmas was after losing my son. One person wrote back to me, having also experienced some recent tragedies. He said,

> *Christmas continues to be bittersweet at times because of all the memories connected to it, and all the moments that will not be until we meet in heaven one day. In a short time I lost my father, mother, and two of my three brothers in unexpected and tragic ways. (One through suicide.) To say the least, Christmas has never been the same. And yet, as a believer, it is such a blessing and comfort to know that we find our hope in Him. And He will heal those sad places in our hearts. Listening to other believers share their story ministers to all of us. I can honestly say I have never felt more loved and comforted by the Lord than in this season through His Word, worship, teaching, and the encouragement of other believers.*

This is a person who understands that while the Christmas of our contemporary culture may be hollow, the reality of Immanuel is a mighty truth, a powerful river of hope, deeper than the deepest pain, and as enduring as eternity. It is "God with us" that gives this grieving soul the strength to go through what he is facing right now.

Before we leave this subject of the promise of Christmas, let's go back again to that incredible night—possibly the greatest, most amazing night in the history of our poor world—when a host of heavenly angels made that dramatic announcement to a motley crew of startled shepherds out in the fields with their flocks.

The Angels and the Promise of Christmas

Since many of us are so familiar with the words and the story, let's read it from a more contemporary translation:

> *There were sheepherders camping in the neighborhood. They had set night watches over their sheep. Suddenly, God's angel stood among them and God's glory blazed around them. They were terrified. The angel said, "Don't be afraid. I'm here to announce a great and joyful event that is meant for everybody, worldwide: A Savior has just been born in David's town, a Savior who is Messiah and Master. This is what you're to look for: a baby wrapped in a blanket and lying in a manger."*
>
> *At once the angel was joined by a huge angelic choir singing God's praises:*

> *Glory to God in the heavenly heights,*
> *Peace to all men and women on earth who please him.*
>
> *As the angel choir withdrew into heaven, the sheepherders talked it over. "Let's get over to Bethlehem as fast as we can and see for ourselves what God has revealed to us." They left, running, and found Mary and Joseph, and the baby lying in the manger. Seeing was believing. They told everyone they met what the angels had said about this child. All who heard the sheepherders were impressed.* (Luke 2:8-18, MSG)

This translation gives us just a little different picture of that night. I've always visualized an event up in the sky somewhere, with the shepherds craning their necks to see—as if it were a fireworks display or an appearance of the aurora borealis. But in this text we read that the angel "suddenly stood among them" and that "God's glory blazed around them."

Boom! Suddenly there was an angel standing in front of them, blazing white-hot like a lightning bolt. They must have shielded their eyes. And then, after his brief announcement, their whole world exploded in beautiful heavenly light, and that lonely field out in the hills was instantly filled with an army of celestial beings, singing God's praises.

It was an illustration of what had already happened.

Heaven had come to earth.

In that moment, earth and heaven were joined.

The shepherds were given a glimpse into eternal glory, and just for a moment, they were privileged to see how heaven itself celebrates Christmas.

What was the hallmark of it all? *Worship.* Singing God's praise. Declaring God's wonders. A Niagara Falls of joy falling over them, sweeping them away in its current.

By the way, Christmas in heaven is way better than Christmas on earth. I mentioned earlier how difficult it was in 2008 for us to celebrate our first Christmas without Christopher. But then the thought occurred to me that December 25, 2008, was Christopher's first Christmas in heaven. Down on earth, we had the privilege of praising a Savior we've never seen. On the Other Side, Christopher was praising the Savior in His immediate presence! So who should have been feeling sorry for whom?

Through the years, ever since Christopher was born, I have been so preprogrammed to shop for him at this time of year. It was hard to stop, even when he had left for heaven. I remember being in a store and seeing a shirt and thinking, *Oh, that shirt would be perfect for Topher. That's what I would get him if he were still here.*

I would have already known what Christopher wanted, because he always told me. Criticize me if you would like, but I always tell my family, "Just tell me exactly what you want, and I will get it for you." And he was always happy to do that, even e-mailing me a link on my computer that would send me to a website and the exact item he wanted.

I don't know how long this will go on, but when I see something really cool in a store, I still find myself thinking, *Oh, I wish Christopher was here. I wish he could see this.* And then I wonder, is he in heaven thinking the same thing about me? *I wish Dad could be up here to see this. This would blow him away.*

I try to picture those things, but it isn't easy. As the music group MercyMe sings, "I can only imagine."

In heaven, it is pure bliss. No twinkling lights on a tree, but the radiant brilliance of the Creator of light. Not painted, metal angels hanging on a tree, but the living, joyful, powerful, holy angels of God. On earth, we have war and constant strife; in heaven, there is perfect harmony and peace. On earth, there is constant friction between family and friends; in heaven, there is feasting and perfect, unspoiled, unshadowed fellowship.

C. S. Lewis put it this way:

All the things that have ever deeply possessed your soul have been but hints of it—tantalizing glimpses, promises never quite fulfilled, echoes that died away just as they caught your ear. . . . It is the secret signature of each soul, the incommunicable and unappeasable want.[1]

The splendor and magnificence of heaven came to earth on that night when the angels stepped through the curtain to appear to the shepherds. Though we may never experience that same event, something supernatural happens when we worship Jesus Christ. We focus on heaven, and in some way that exceeds our understanding, we actually occupy the same ground as heaven. Listen to how Paul described it to the church at Colosse:

Since you became alive again, so to speak, when Christ arose from the dead, now set your sights on the rich treasures and joys of heaven where he sits beside God in the place of honor and power. Let heaven fill your thoughts; don't spend your time worrying about things down here. (Colossians 3:1-2, TLB)

In other words, set your mind on Jesus Christ and the joys of heaven, and some of that joy will touch your life here on earth.

What, then, was the essence of the angels' message that night to the shepherds?

The Message of the Angels
1. "Don't be afraid."

The angel said, "Don't be afraid." (Luke 2:10, MSG)

We read those words, but there is a lot to be afraid of today, isn't there? We are afraid of the future. We are afraid of terrorism.

We are afraid of what is happening in our economy. We are afraid for our nation, so obviously going into decline. We are afraid of what is going on in popular culture, with depravity and twisted values becoming more and more mainstream. We're afraid for our families in such a debased, degraded culture. We're afraid of rogue nations using nuclear weapons against us. We're afraid for our marriages, with all the stresses and strains that seek to tear us apart. We're afraid of the dark world our little grandchildren are coming into.

There is so much to be afraid of. But the angels said, "Don't be afraid."

Did you know that in the Bible, the phrase "don't be afraid" is used 365 times? That means there is one "don't be afraid" for every day of the year. Fear always robs us of joy. It's hard to be afraid when you are joyful, and it's hard to be joyful when you are afraid.

A friend recently told me about his experience in a worship service. As the music was soaring and people around him were lifting their hands in praise, the Lord spoke to his heart and said, "You *can't* worship Me. Your insides are completely frozen with fear. Let Me deal with your fear, and then you will be able to praise Me." So that is just what he did. He released those fears to the Lord and felt them melt away in that time of worship. And then he could really worship the Lord, not just go through the motions.

So . . . *don't be afraid*. And why?

2. The Messiah has come.

A Savior has just been born in David's town, a Savior who is Messiah and Master. (verse 11, MSG)

Why should the shepherds let go of their fear? Because Jesus had come. Messiah had come. And He is the answer to every fear, no matter what it might be!

The angels were saying, "Your prayers are answered. Messiah has come. He is going to live a perfect life, and He will voluntarily die on a cross and bear your sins and the sins of the world. He will rise again bodily from the dead three days later and ascend to heaven as your Representative and Advocate before the throne of God."

And from our point of view, the Messiah not only has come, but He is *coming*. He will return to earth, first for His church, and then to rule and reign on earth and set everything right once again.

Do you ever wonder about your future? *That* is your future — to rule and reign alongside King Jesus forever.

3. Because Messiah has come — and will come again — rejoice!

I'm here to announce a great and joyful event that is meant for everybody. (verse 10, MSG)

There is so much to be joyful about at this time of year that has nothing whatsoever to do with politics, the economy, the stock market, or what you receive under the Christmas tree.

The key is spending time in God's presence. In the psalms we are told, "In Your presence is fullness of joy" (Psalm 16:11). Another translation reads, "You have let me experience the joys of life and the exquisite pleasures of your own eternal presence" (TLB).

And by the way, did you know that being joyful is good for your health? We are told in Proverbs 15:13, "A happy heart makes the face cheerful, but heartache crushes the spirit" (NIV). Proverbs 17:22 says, "A cheerful heart is good medicine, but a broken spirit saps a person's strength" (NLT).

What am I suggesting here? That you walk around with a fake smile plastered on your face, saying "praise the Lord" under your breath 24/7? No, I'm not. In fact, there is a place for sorrow, a place for mourning, a place for tears. We can acknowledge our heartaches and disappointments just like anyone else. But underneath it all, like two mighty underground rivers, there can be joy and hope. And that inner confidence will eventually bubble its way to the surface, even in the darkest of times.

This is such a powerful magnet to the nonbeliever. When a Christian can genuinely and authentically rejoice during times of suffering and pain, it is a powerful testimony for Jesus Christ.

Friedrich Nietzsche, the atheist and German philosopher,

once said to some Christians, "If you want me to believe in your redeemer, you're going to have to look more redeemed." A lot of people don't look redeemed at all; they have a sour disposition — as though they had been baptized in lemon juice rather than in water. Do you look redeemed?

You might say, "But, Greg, you really don't understand. I'm having a hard time this Christmas. There are problems in my life, problems in my marriage, problems with my kids, and problems with my health. My finances are in trouble. My best friend has turned against me. How can I rejoice in Christmas?"

I understand that. But I'm not talking about rejoicing in Christmas. I am talking about rejoicing in Christ. Christ has come. That is how we can have joy.

One of the most beautiful songs we hear at this time of year is "I Heard the Bells on Christmas Day," written by the famous American poet Henry Wadsworth Longfellow. The story behind it is very compelling. In 1860 Longfellow was at the peak of his success as a poet, known and celebrated throughout the nation. There was a buoyant optimism in the air that year as Abraham Lincoln was elected to the presidency, giving hope to many. In a matter of months, however, things turned very dark — both for the young nation of America and for Longfellow personally.

The Civil War began the next year, with the sickening prospect of brothers fighting against brothers and even fathers against sons. It was our country's greatest trial. And adding to that, Longfellow faced a great personal heartbreak: His wife was burned to death in a tragic accident in their home. In his attempt to save her, he too was severely burned. In fact, he was so badly hurt that he wasn't even able to attend her funeral.

In his diary for Christmas 1861, he wrote, "How inexpressibly sad are the holidays." The following year, the toll of war dead began to mount in a ghastly, almost incomprehensible way. That year Longfellow wrote, "'A Merry Christmas,' say the children. There is no more for me." His son had run away unexpectedly and joined the army—only to be returned home with severe wounds. That following Christmas, things were so bleak that the great poet put no entry at all in his diary.

Nevertheless, he wanted to pull out of his despair. So he tried to capture the joy of the season in verse. That poem became a familiar Christmas song for generations. He began it like this:

I heard the bells on Christmas Day
Their old familiar carols play,
And wild and sweet the words repeat
Of peace on earth, good will to men.

But then he stopped and thought about the condition of his country. The terrible Battle of Gettysburg had recently occurred, and things were looking so dark. Longfellow wondered how he could write about the joy of the season. He continued on:

And in despair I bowed my head
"There is no peace on earth," I said,
"For hate is strong and mocks the song
Of peace on earth, good will to men."

But then Longfellow, catching an eternal perspective, began to see his life and circumstances from God's point of view, leading him to conclude:

Then pealed the bells more loud and deep:
"God is not dead, nor doth He sleep;
The wrong shall fail, the right prevail
With peace on earth, good will to men."

We have to get our perspective right. Mankind *never* will bring peace on earth. The United Nations *never* will persuade nations to agree with one another or stop fighting. You can "visualize world peace" all you like, but it won't occur until the Prince of Peace Himself takes His rightful throne. Don't buy into the utopian dream of any politician, any political philosophy, or any political party bringing peace. We never will see real justice and lasting peace until Christ Himself comes back and establishes His kingdom on earth.

That doesn't mean we shouldn't hope for peace or work for peace or pray for peace. But it does mean that we need to be realistic in our expectations. As long as human beings are in charge, there always will be friction and conflict.

The promise of Christmas is no promise at all apart from the Christ of Christmas.

What You Don't Have, and What You Do

There may be some things you wish you had this Christmas. You may not have the resources to give what you would like to your loved ones and friends. You may be struggling with some physical problem and have ongoing pain that keeps you on the edge of discouragement and distress. You may be hurting over a broken relationship. You may have a loved one who was with you last year but won't be with you this year.

Those are things you don't have.

But let me tell you the things that you do have.

Look back at Luke 2:11: "For there is born to you this day in the city of David a Savior, who is Christ the Lord." The fact is, you have a Savior, you have a Christ, and you have a Lord.

You have a Savior.

You have a Savior who came to save you from the power and penalty of sin. You were separated from God, and there was nothing you ever could have done to satisfy His righteous demands. Not in a billion years. But God placed His wrath on Jesus Christ, who died in our place. And when we put our faith in Him, we have the strong assurance that we will not die. Oh yes, our body will die (to be resurrected later). But we will live on in eternity. We have God's own guarantee that we will go to heaven when we leave this earth. We have a Savior. That is a lot to be thankful for this year.

You have a Christ.

The word *Christ* means "anointed one." Another word that we use is Messiah. Jesus was the fulfillment of God's promises to send His Son as the Messiah. It was a reminder to all of us that God keeps His promises.

And what has God promised to you? More than I could relate in this book—or a dozen books. He has promised that you will never be alone. He said, "I will never leave you nor forsake you" (Hebrews 13:5). He has promised that He can work all things together for good to those who love Him (see Romans 8:28). He has promised that He will come again and receive us unto Himself (see John 14:3). And He has promised that we will see our loved ones again.[2]

You have a Savior. You have a Christ. And lastly . . .

You have a Lord.

I'm so glad for this! I am no longer in control of my own life. I don't have to be the one to call the shots. I don't have to run around day and night ironing out every little detail. I have a Lord! I have a King! I've never been more aware of that fact than I am right now. It's not that I ever thought I really had control in my life; it's just that I have become more acutely aware of how little control I ever had!

The Bible tells us, "A man's heart plans his way, but the LORD directs his steps" (Proverbs 16:9). I'm so happy about that. I don't want to direct my own steps, because I'll get it wrong every time. I want God to direct me, even if I don't understand where He's leading me.

God is in control of my life, and He is in control of your life as well if you have put your faith in Christ. He will direct you in the way that you should go, and He will protect you and watch over you as you go in that way. And then, when your work has been completed, He will welcome you into heaven. That is our hope.

So don't look to Christmas—the holiday, the square on the calendar—to meet your expectations or fulfill your longings or bring you fulfillment. Look to Christ.

The truth is, we feel let down and disappointed because of false expectations as to what Christmas should be.

Some people don't mind taking time off to commemorate

the birth of Jesus, but that is the extent of it. He is all right as long as He stays in that manger as a baby. They don't like the idea of Jesus growing into a man and telling them to turn from their sin, dying on a cross for them, and rising again from the dead.

There are many people who essentially say, "I'm okay with God as long as He stays out of my life." They might have a bumper sticker on their car that says, "God is my copilot." That's nice. But the fact of the matter is, you shouldn't even be in the cockpit. God doesn't want to be your copilot; He wants to be in control of your life. But that is where people want God. They want Him in the cockpit in case of emergency, and that is about the extent of their faith. These people wrongly think they make their own luck and are the captains of their own ships, the masters of their own destinies.

Escaping the Trap

Some look down on Christians and say, "You people are a bunch of automatons, marching in lockstep. You want to do the will of God. Well, fine. But I want to do the will of me. I'm in control of my own life. I decide what direction I am going to take."

I have news for them.

Life doesn't work that way.

People who reject Jesus Christ are not in control of their own lives, nor are they making their own luck. According to the Bible, those outside of Christ are under the control of someone else. And that someone else is Satan.

In 2 Timothy 2:25-26, Paul wrote these words to believers:

Be humble when you are trying to teach those who are mixed up concerning the truth. For if you talk meekly and courteously to them, they are more likely, with God's help, to turn away from their wrong ideas and believe what is true. Then they will come to their senses and escape from Satan's trap of slavery to sin, which he uses to catch them whenever he likes, *and then they can begin doing the will of God.* (TLB, *emphasis added*)

You don't realize this when you're a nonbeliever. You imagine yourself to be in charge of your own life. You convince yourself that you are calling all the shots. But it's strange. Have you ever noticed how most nonbelievers do the same things? They get caught up in the same miserable lifestyle. And then one day, by God's grace, you wake up and look around you and say, "What is this? What am I doing here? How did I get to this place? I hate this life."

That is what happened in Jesus' story of the lost son (see Luke 15:11-32). This was the young man who took his share of his dad's inheritance, left for Vegas (or something like that), blew all his money, and ended up as a farm laborer, feeding pigs in a pigpen. As he was watching the fat hogs grub around in the muck for scraps, he found himself thinking that some of those scraps were looking pretty good.

That is when it hit him. The Bible says that he "came to his senses" (verse 17, NLT). And then he said, "I will arise and go to my father" (verse 18).

That's what happened to me as a young man. I started looking around at my life and thought, *This stinks. I'm sick of these stupid parties. I'm tired of drinking and drugs. I can't stand all of these cliques and the way these people live. I've had enough of all the backstabbing and hypocrisy. There has to be something better.*

Those thoughts, that inner restlessness and dissatisfaction, sent me on a quest to find purpose and meaning. I thought, *Surely there's more to life than this.* The adult world that I'd been exposed to certainly wasn't the world where I wanted to live. The empty, unhappy lives of my friends and peers didn't appeal to me either.

So I started looking. My search led me to hearing the gospel and giving my life to Christ. Then I started coming to church and hanging out with God's people, and I began seeing the reality I had been searching for all along. I found a place where love and brotherhood and joy could be experienced—not because you were high on something, but because it came through a relationship with God.

Jesus filled all the longings in my life that I thought never could be filled.

He is still in the business of doing that.

He, and He alone, is the real promise of Christmas.

10

BE READY FOR HIS COMING

For all the effort our secular world puts into stamping out the memory and traditions of Christmas, you can still see it coming.

You've probably seen the telltale signs in your town and in your neighborhood. The lights are going up on houses. These days, you see more of those giant Frosty the Snowman and Rudolph the Reindeer inflatables. Now and then, and not as often as in days gone by, you will see a manger scene in someone's yard.

You see Christmas trees on top of cars and traffic backing up around the malls, and you can throw out your back from lifting your morning newspaper, stuffed with a thousand slick advertising pieces. And then, of course, there are the nonstop commercials, promoting every article or service under the sun as a Christmas gift.

I was watching a cartoon with my granddaughter Stella the other day, and after one of the toy commercials, she said, "Papa, can you get that for me? Will you get that for me?"

"I don't know, Stella," I said. "I don't think I like that last toy. Let me find one that's really cool. If I see a cool toy, maybe I'll get it."

Then the next toy ad came on, and she said, "Papa, was that cool enough?"

Ah . . . the pressure is on! Everyone on all sides is pushing us to get out there and spend our money in order to "celebrate" this season. I don't think it is possible to miss the fact that Christmas is here.

As I have said in this book, however, many people did miss that first Christmas, when Jesus was born in Bethlehem. In fact, most people in the world missed it.

Of course, there weren't the telltale signs we have today. There were no reindeer on anyone's front lawn back then. No Christmas carols to hear quite yet. No brightly colored lights hanging from the little huts that people were living in. No sales at the downtown market. No brightly wrapped presents and so forth. And most likely, children didn't find it hard at all to sleep that night, because . . . it was a night like any other.

Or so it seemed.

But it is not as though the people of Israel didn't have signs and signals that something special was in the air. Godly men and women must have sensed that the coming of the Messiah was near.

We have already spoken of godly Simeon, who had God's personal word on it:

> *And behold, there was a man in Jerusalem whose name was Simeon, and this man was just and devout, waiting for the Consolation of Israel, and the Holy Spirit was upon him. And it had been revealed to him by the Holy Spirit that he would not see death before he had seen the Lord's Christ. (Luke 2:25-26)*

When he saw the baby Jesus in the temple with Mary and Joseph, the Holy Spirit whispered to him that this was the One.

About the same time, they were approached by an elderly saint named Anna, who also recognized Baby Jesus as the Messiah, and "she gave thanks to the Lord, and spoke of Him to all those who looked for redemption in Jerusalem" (Luke 2:38).

Right after the disciple Philip had met Jesus, he hurried off to tell his fellow townsman Nathanael about it, saying, "We have found the very person Moses and the prophets wrote about! His name is Jesus, the son of Joseph from Nazareth" (John 1:45, NLT).

The woman at the well in Sychar, even though she was a Samaritan, was also looking for the Messiah. Before she recognized Jesus for who He was, she said, "'I know that Messiah' (called Christ) 'is coming. When he comes, he will explain everything to us'" (John 4:25, NIV).

There's no doubt about it: Even after 400 years of silence, there were those in Israel who had stayed on their tiptoes, watching and waiting for the appearance of Messiah.

The Hebrew prophets had clearly foretold the fact that a Savior was coming, that He indeed would be the Messiah, that He would be born of a virgin, that He would be a direct descendent of David, and that He would be born in the tiny village of Bethlehem.

For the most part, however, people missed those signs.

Why? Because they weren't paying attention.

Life was difficult under Roman occupation, and most people just plodded along, trying to make a living and stay out of trouble with the authorities. The Jewish leaders and scholars, though their heads were filled with biblical content, had become completely absorbed in the minutiae of all the extra laws, regulations, and traditions that had been added to the Law over the generations. In fact, they were so distracted that they didn't recognize the Messiah when He was standing right in front of them.

Things were spiritually dark for Israel in those days. No one had seen an angel or heard from a prophet or witnessed a miracle in living memory. Demons were abroad in the land, possessing men and women in frightening ways and inflicting diseases.

But things were ripe for the arrival of Messiah — and the godly people in the land sensed it and watched for it.

Sadly, however, many people in Israel were spiritually asleep when God visited them that first Christmas. It is pretty much the same when we look at our own culture today. Yes, we celebrate Christmas, but it is so easy to forget about Christ.

But you and I can make sure that we are ready when He returns to the earth as He has promised. Jesus Christ, born in the manger in Bethlehem, crucified on the cross of Calvary, risen again from the dead, is coming back again.

This may not be a popular topic of discussion, but that doesn't make it any less true. Some people don't want to talk about the Rapture or the Second Coming and instead shrug it off as a fad or as something of little importance. That is just what the apostle Peter said people would do:

> I want to remind you that in the last days there will come scoffers who will do every wrong they can think of and laugh at the truth. This will be their line of argument: "So Jesus promised to come back, did he? Then where is he? He'll never come! Why, as far back as anyone can remember, everything has remained exactly as it was since the first day of creation." (2 Peter 3:3-4, TLB)

Those who have been watching and waiting, however, know that He will come soon—and we don't want to miss that! He came right on schedule the first time, and He will come right on schedule the second time. The book of Galatians tells us, "But when the time had fully come, God sent his Son, born of a woman" (Galatians 4:4, NIV).

Jesus was born in Bethlehem when the time was just right. He wasn't early, and He wasn't late. And it will be the same way when He comes back again. He will come when the time is just right, the time set by His Father.

For those whose eyes are open, for those who are alert and watching, the signs and signals of His soon return are everywhere. There are 260 chapters in the New Testament, and Christ's return is mentioned no less than 318 times in these chapters. It is a recurring theme in the Bible. In John 14:3, Jesus Himself said, "And if I go and prepare a place for you, I will come again and receive you to Myself; that where I am, there you may be also."

In Mark 8:38, Jesus spoke of the time when He would come "in the glory of His Father with the holy angels."

Sometimes, as we watch things going from bad to worse in our cities, in our nation, and in our world, we may find ourselves wondering, *Lord, are You really paying attention to planet Earth? Do You realize how bad it has become?* The answer is yes, He is fully aware of everything that is happening (and an infinite number of things that you are not aware of).

Regarding the timing of His coming, Jesus said, "But of that day and hour no one knows" (Matthew 24:36). Translate that out of the original language, and He says, "But of that day and hour no one knows." Explaining it carefully, it means, "But of that day and hour no one knows."

So if you hear some teacher on the radio or preacher on TV say that he knows the day of the Lord's return, go ahead and change the station, flip the channel. He doesn't know what he is talking about, because Jesus says, *"No one knows."* Period.

But if we can't know the specific date, we can discern the *season* that we are in. Jesus said in Matthew 16:2-3, "You know the saying, 'Red sky at night means fair weather tomorrow; red sky in the morning means foul weather all day.' You know how to interpret the weather signs in the sky, but you don't know how to interpret the signs of the times!" (NLT).

Early this morning, it was raining outside my house. How did I know that? Well, it was like this: I walked outside, and it rained on me. By the way, bald men are always first to know when it's raining. I will be walking down the street with my wife, and I will say, "It is raining."

She will say, "No, it's not."

But she has so much hair, she wouldn't know if it was a hurricane.

I will reply, "Yes, it *is* raining. I feel the drops on my head!"

No, we can't know the day or the hour of Christ's return, but we can learn to read the signs of the times. And those signs have been saying consistently and clearly that the time for our Lord's return is near.

You might ask, "What are those signs?"

I could write a book on that. (In fact, I have.) First of all, I would mention the regathering of the nation Israel into their ancient homeland. That is not only a sign, it is a *supersign*. God predicted that the nation of Israel would be dispersed to the four corners of the earth, and that in the last days, they would be regathered and become a nation once again, surrounded by hostile enemies. And that is exactly what has happened with Israel today.

There is no historical precedent for such a thing happening with any other nation in the world. But against all odds, Israel reformed as a nation on May 14, 1948, after having reestablished themselves in their homeland. The Bible tells us that not only will Israel have hostile, dangerous enemies, but there will be weapons with the capacity to destroy our planet. The book of Revelation and other Scriptures offer vivid descriptions of catastrophic devastation. And today we have the technology at our fingertips to fulfill some of these terrifying Bible prophecies.

I read recently that the nation of Iran, a sworn enemy of Israel, now claims the ability to produce yellow-cake uranium, which means they are a step closer to producing their own nuclear weapons. What's more, that nation has threatened to use nuclear weapons against the nation they call "the little Satan," or Israel. The "great Satan" they refer to is, of course, the United States of America.

These are clear signs of the times, yet many look on these developments and events—including people you work with, go to school with, or live next door to—with complete indifference. There are people today who have a better handle on how to prepare for a Christmas celebration than how to prepare for the return of Jesus Christ.

What Are We to Do?

What are we to do in light of the fact that Christ is coming again? We don't have to wonder or be in the dark. Jesus told us:

> *Be dressed for service and keep your lamps burning, as though you were waiting for your master to return from the wedding feast. Then you will be ready to open the door and let him in the moment he arrives and knocks. The servants who are ready and waiting for his return will be rewarded. I tell you the truth, he himself will seat them, put on an apron, and serve them as they sit and eat! He may come in the middle of the night or just before dawn. But whenever he comes, he will reward the servants who are ready.*
>
> *Understand this: If a homeowner knew exactly when a burglar was coming, he would not permit his house to be broken into. You also must be ready all the time, for the Son of Man will come when least expected. (Luke 12:35-40, NLT)*

When we read an account like this, it might be hard for us to grasp sometimes, because it is relating to a long-ago and faraway culture, back in biblical times. What Jesus is describing is a classic first-century Jewish wedding. Unlike our weddings today, a first-century Hebrew wedding would last *days* rather than hours. It was an extended time of celebration. One of the fun elements was the fact that you didn't know when the groom was coming. The bridal party would be assembled, the bridesmaids would be prepared, and the groomsmen would be ready.

But where was the groom?

With no warning, an announcement would be made: *"The groom is coming!"*

If you were asleep or off doing this or that, you might miss the ceremony. It might come in the middle of the night, or it might come early in the morning at first light. You simply had to *be* ready and *stay* ready, sleeping in your wedding clothes if you had to. The groom suddenly would be in your midst, and the ceremony would begin.

Jesus was saying, "That is how it will be when I return. Be ready. Be alert. Don't be overly preoccupied with other things." The New King James version says, "Let your waist be girded and your lamps burning" (verse 35).

What does it mean to have your waist girded? Back in those days, they wore long, flowing robes with a belt. When they wanted to cinch up their robe for easier movement, they would tuck it into their belt. This belt also would have objects attached. For instance, they would sometimes carry an extra flask of oil for their lamp. (It would be like having extra alkaline batteries for your flashlight.) Their lamp was saucerlike, filled with oil and a floating wick. When your oil got low, you would pull out your little flask and replenish your lamp.

Jesus was saying to keep your robe cinched up and tucked into your belt, so that you could move fast when you need to. In other words, put those fresh batteries in that flashlight. Gas up your car. Have your cell phone charged to the max. Be ready to roll at a moment's notice.

And that is how we are to be in anticipation of our Lord's return.

When Christ comes, you won't have time to change anything. You won't be able to say, "Well, I need to wrap a couple of things up first."

No, there will be no time. It will occur in a millisecond—"in the twinkling of an eye," as 1 Corinthians 15:52 says. So you just need to be ready and stay ready. Because you could be walking from the kitchen into the living room and suddenly find yourself swept up into the clouds. You could be having a conversation with a friend, and suddenly you're with the Lord in the air. That is how fast the Rapture will happen, and it could take place at any moment. There is nothing left on the prophetic calendar that has to happen before Jesus returns for His church.

Jesus made an interesting statement in Luke 12:38: "If he should come in the second watch, or come in the third watch, and find them so, blessed are those servants."

What does that mean? Back in those days, they divided the night into four watches, or shifts. The first watch was from six to nine. The second was from nine to twelve. The third was from twelve to three. And the fourth watch of the night included the time just before dawn.

So Jesus was saying, in effect, "If I come later than you had originally expected, be ready." It is another reminder to us that Christ will come right on time — *His* time. The apostle Peter said, "The Lord is not slow in keeping his promise, as some understand slowness. He is patient with you, not wanting anyone to perish, but everyone to come to repentance" (2 Peter 3:9, NIV).

I believe that Jesus Christ is waiting for that last person to believe, so we can all go to heaven. Who is that last person? Wouldn't it be nice to know? I think we might be tempted to pressure that person just a bit, don't you? We might say to them, "Hey, are you going to get saved or what?"

Whoever it may be, when that last person says yes to Jesus, we all will be caught up into the clouds to meet the Lord in the air.

So what are we supposed to be doing until the Lord comes back? There are several things, according to Luke 12.

1. We are to be watching for Him.

Blessed are those servants whom the master, when he comes, will find watching. (Luke 12:37)

This doesn't mean that we are to stand around like idiots, staring into the sky. To *watch* simply means to be alert and aware. For instance, when I read the newspaper or go to a news website, I'm always thinking about world news and national news in terms of the signs of the times. So I am not just seeing another conflict in the Middle East or reading about an economic meltdown in Europe or noting that North Korea has threatened to use its nuclear weapons. I'm looking for things that might point to biblical signs and indicate that the day of the Lord's return is near.

Jesus said, "Now when these things begin to happen, look up and lift up your heads, because your redemption draws near" (Luke 21:28). The Bible also says, "He will appear a second time, not to bear sin, but to bring salvation to those who are waiting for him" (Hebrews 9:28, NIV).

So be watching.

2. We are to be ready to go.

As Christmas approaches, most of us have a to-do list. We want to get the house decorated, the shopping done, and maybe a menu planned for when company arrives. That means *before*

December 24! It won't help to get ready for Christmas after Christmas is over. So here is a word to the wise, especially if you're a guy: Don't let Christmas Eve come as a revelation to you. Make sure you have thought through what you're getting for your wife or your girlfriend. You will have a happier Christmas if you are ready!

Referring to the coming of Jesus, Scripture is saying to us, be ready to go. Have your bags packed. Have your shirt sleeves rolled up. Have your comfortable shoes on. Be ready to depart at a moment's notice.

This is the question we need to ask ourselves: *Am I ready?*

You don't want to be engaged in some activity that would make you ashamed if Jesus suddenly returned. It is an interesting question to ask yourself periodically: *Is this place I'm about to go to, is this thing I'm ready to do something that I would be ashamed of or embarrassed to be involved with if Jesus were to come back?* If the answer to that question is yes, then I would suggest that you not do it.

If you really believe that Christ could return at any moment, it will have a practical impact on the way that you live. In 1 John 3, the apostle said,

> Beloved, now we are children of God; and it has not yet been revealed what we shall be, but we know that when He is revealed, we shall be like Him, for we shall see Him as He is. And everyone who has this hope in Him purifies himself, just as He is pure. (verses 2-3)

In other words, the stronger I hold to the truth about Christ's any-moment return, the more it will impact how I live my life.

Have you ever noticed how people behave differently when a uniformed police officer enters the room? I have a few friends who are cops, and I was meeting with one for coffee the other day. So we walked into a little coffee place together, and the whole atmosphere of the room changed. People began confessing stuff to him: "I really wasn't speeding that much on my way over here." He just laughed.

Or have you noticed how the flow of traffic changes when a state patrol car merges onto the highway? Everyone slows down, and no one wants to be the one to pass him! We alter our activity, because we are aware of the presence of an authority figure. In the same way, knowing that Jesus could merge into our world at literally any second ought to affect the way we live, what we do, and what we say.

3. We should not only be ready for His return, but we should anxiously await it.

And you yourselves be like men who wait for their master, when he will return from the wedding, that when he comes and knocks they may open to him immediately. (Luke 12:36)

Have you ever dreaded the arrival of someone at your house? Do you remember what that felt like and how you didn't even want to answer the door?

Then again, have you ever looked forward to someone's arrival, and before they could even knock, you opened the door? That is how we should be when we think of the return of Jesus: looking forward to that moment with anticipation and joy, not dreading it at all.

In the book of Revelation, in the very last two verses of the Bible, Jesus said, "Surely I am coming quickly." And the response of every true Christian will be, "Amen. Even so, come, Lord Jesus!"

Anything that would prevent us from answering in this way is out of place in our lives. Anything that would make it difficult for us to say, "Come quickly, Lord Jesus!" is really spiritual weakness and a danger area to us.

4. We are not only to be waiting, but we are also to be working.

Blessed is that servant whom his master will find so doing when he comes. (Luke 12:43)

If watching is the evidence of faith, then working is the evidence of faith in action. Watching for the Lord's return will help us prepare our own lives, but working will assure that we bring others with us. We should be using the days and years of our lives to serve the Lord and to look for every opportunity to tell people about Jesus.

This is a happy way to live. Luke 12:37 says, "Blessed are those servants whom the master, when he comes, will find watching." This verse could be translated, "*Oh, how happy* are those servants."

Watching daily for the Lord's return isn't a miserable, repressive, confining way to live; it is a happy, joyful, purposeful way to live.

So yes, Christmas is coming, and the signs are all around us.

But the fact is that it's just a holiday. Most of us quickly will forget the gifts we receive. In fact, most of us can't remember the gifts we received last year. Christmas will come and go, whether we are ready for it or not. But when it comes to Jesus Christ returning to earth, being ready couldn't be more important. People may have missed the first Christmas, but we don't want to miss His return. He is coming for those who are watching and waiting.

So don't just be ready for Christmas this year; be ready for Christ Himself.

GOD WITH US

Children's toys have become unbelievably more complex and elaborate than the toys of previous generations.

Back in 1960, I remember asking—begging—for a "Mr. Machine" for Christmas. At that time, this was a toy on the very edge of technological sophistication. And I was wildly excited to discover that I actually had it waiting for me under the tree that year.

As I remember, it didn't plug in and didn't have any batteries. By winding a large metal key on Mr. Machine's back, however, he would roll forward, legs and arms moving, bell ringing, while he opened his mouth and squawked. You could rotate a little wheel behind the toy to make it run in a circle or curve instead of moving in a straight line.

And that was about it.

I remember thinking that it looked so cool and futuristic, and I felt pretty happy about it — until my buddy came over with *his* new toy.

I had never seen anything like it. It was a little plastic battery-operated scuba diver, outfitted with dual tanks just like Lloyd Bridges on the old *Sea Hunt* TV series. When you turned it on, the legs kicked. You could put it in your bathtub or wading pool, and it sank to the bottom with bubbles coming out the top.

It was absolutely the edgiest technology I had ever seen. And suddenly I wasn't so happy with my Mr. Machine. I wanted a plastic scuba diver, too.

The funny thing is that as you get older, things really don't change much. What is that old saying? "The only difference between men and boys is the price of their toys." And that is why Christmas is such a letdown for so many people, children and otherwise. There is such a buildup surrounding the giving and getting of presents.

Here is the basic problem: No matter what you receive, no matter how high the price tag or elaborate the technology, "things" will always disappoint you. If that is what Christmas is all about to you, the holiday will always be a synonym for disappointment.

That is why all the people who work so tirelessly to take Jesus Christ out of Christmas will receive exactly what they want: a meaningless holiday with an emphasis on material possessions and acquiring stuff.

If, however, you want to have the merriest Christmas of all, if you want to experience Christmas the way it was meant to be experienced, you need to understand and embrace the essential message of the season. Which is simply this: *Immanuel.* God is with us.

The first chapter of Matthew lays it out for us:

All this was done that it might be fulfilled which was spoken by the Lord through the prophet, saying: "Behold, the virgin shall be with child, and bear a Son, and they shall call His name Immanuel," which is translated, "God with us." (verses 22-23)

Did Joseph and Mary really have any concept at all about the Child who was to enter their lives? When Mary (probably no more than a young teenager) gave birth to her Baby in that inhospitable place, wrapped Him in strips of rags, and placed Him in a manger, possibly in the back of some cave near Bethlehem, did she grasp who He was? Did she know that the Child she nursed and held in her arms was the Savior of the world? Did she have any comprehension that her little one was *God* in human form?

Most of us have heard the contemporary song "Mary, Did You Know?":

Did you know that your baby boy has walked where angels trod?
When you kiss your little baby, you have kissed the face of God.

Did she? Did she know? Did she understand that this was Immanuel—God with us?

What a staggering thought that is. Not just for Mary, but for any of us. "God with us" is the very essence of the Christian experience. All other religions basically lay out things that you must *do* to somehow reach God or make it to heaven or achieve nirvana or simply escape wrath. You must do this and this and this and this. And if you do it all perfectly, then maybe you will gain the approval of God or reach the outskirts of heaven.

In contrast to all the other religions of the world, Christianity doesn't say "do," it says "done"! Our salvation was accomplished by God Himself, for us.

How? It was because of Immanuel, God with us, the God who became a man and took our penalty on Himself.

Christmas is a lonely time of year for many people. Some people dread the month of December, wishing they could skip right from Thanksgiving to New Year's Day. Maybe there are parents with an empty nest who miss the hustle and bustle of Christmases past. Maybe someone has lost a spouse to death, and memories of Christmas only seem to make the pain and desolation harder to bear. Or perhaps a marriage broke up or has been strained, and all the holiday celebrations seem empty and sad.

Is that a description of you? Is this a time of anxiety or sadness for you? Are you lonely and feel as though you have no one at all?

What is loneliness? It is a painful sense of being unwanted, unloved, unneeded, uncared for, and maybe even unnecessary. Studies have shown that one of the main reasons people commit suicide is because deep down inside, they are lonely.

That is why the name Immanuel is so inexpressibly powerful.

GOD . . . IS . . . WITH . . . YOU.

He didn't just say that; He *named* Himself that.

You are not alone, and that is what God would have you understand right now.

He Understands Your Sorrows

Did it ever cross your mind that Jesus of Nazareth might have been the loneliest Man who ever lived?

You say, "Greg, what are you talking about? Jesus had His disciples."

Yes, He did.

But the Bible tells us that "even in his own land and among his own people, the Jews, he was not accepted. Only a few would welcome and receive him" (John 1:11, TLB). The Old Testament prophet, writing of Jesus' life, said of Him, "We despised him and rejected him—a man of sorrows, acquainted with bitterest grief. We turned our backs on him and looked the other way when he went by. He was despised, and we didn't care" (Isaiah 53:3, TLB).

Those disciples of His couldn't even stay awake to watch with Him in the greatest crisis of His life. And when a murderous mob descended on the Lord, they all took off to save their own skins, leaving Him to be condemned and abused and die.

On the cross, with His life slipping away inch by agonizing inch as He bore the weight of all the sins of all time on His shoulders, Jesus even experienced a separation from God the Father. He called out from the cross, "My God, My God, why have You forsaken Me?" (Matthew 27:46).

Jesus knows all about loneliness. He can be with you in a special way if you are feeling lonely this Christmas. His name is Immanuel. God with *you*.

Here is what Jesus has promised to every man or woman, boy or girl who has ever put their faith in Him: "I will never leave you nor forsake you. . . . And be sure of this: I am with you always, even to the end of the age" (Hebrews 13:5, NKJV; Matthew 28:20, NLT).

That is the bottom line of this book and the bottom line of life itself. Jesus, and Jesus alone, will meet your needs — not Christmas presents, not even family and friends. People, even good people who love you, will let you down in some way, shape, or form. You and I have let down people, and we have been let down by people in turn. But Jesus never will let you down. He alone is the answer to loneliness, and He will live with you, beside you, and within you.

Without question, that is one of the most remarkable teachings in all of the Bible, that somehow, some way, but in literal fact, Christ Himself enters into the human heart and *lives* there.

The Bible clearly teaches this, whether we are able to wrap our minds around it or not. In fact, our Lord said in John 14:23, "If anyone loves Me, he will keep My word; and My Father will love him, and We will come to him and make Our home with him."

Don't let this sound like a bunch of religious jargon to you. It's as real as the chair you are sitting in right now, as real as the air you are drawing into your lungs. Jesus is saying, "My Father and I want to come and set up house with you. We want to live inside of you."

No, I don't understand it very well, either. But I know this: No matter what, I am not alone in life, and I *never will be* alone in life. And neither will you, no matter what you are going through right now, no matter what difficulty or crisis or heartbreak you might be facing, no matter what impossibility looms on the path ahead of you.

God is with you — not in an abstract, theoretical way, but in fact, in truth, and in person. Remember the verse we quoted earlier from Isaiah 43? "When you pass through the waters, I will be with you . . . when you walk through the fire, you shall not be burned" (verse 3).

Are you going through a river of difficulty this Christmas? Maybe you find yourself in a fire of oppression. Remember, you are not alone. God is with you.

Maybe your marriage has been badly bruised—or has fallen apart completely this year. Perhaps your children have forgotten about you. But God is with you, and He has *not* forgotten about you. Maybe you find yourself isolated in a hospital room or a convalescent home or a prison cell. I get letters from people writing me from these places all the time. But you are not alone in that place. God is with you as well. That is the essential message of Christmas—that God is with us.

Have you asked Jesus into your life?

Revelation 3:20 is one of my favorite verses in all the Bible. In that verse, Jesus says, "Behold, I stand at the door and knock. If anyone hears My voice and opens the door, I will come in to him and dine with him, and he with Me."

The problem with this translation is that it sounds too formal. Who says "behold" anymore? When you knock on someone's door, you usually don't say, "BEHOLD!"

I'm not making fun of the statement of Jesus; I'm just saying the translation doesn't relate very well. So, to bring it into modern vernacular, Jesus is saying, "I'm at the door. Open up. Hey, it's your Friend out here."

Yes, that's a very loose paraphrase. But you get the idea. What is Jesus saying? He's saying, "I want to come into your life. I want to be a part of everything that you're doing. Let's have a meal together. I want to spend time with you."

Personally, I don't enjoy eating with people I don't know. I keep thinking, *Maybe they're trying to sell me something.* And I just can't relax. When it comes to eating a meal, I only want to eat with someone who is a friend or family member or someone I'm comfortable with. I want to eat my food and steal some of theirs too. That's how you know you are a really good friend — when you can take the food off their plate without asking.

Jesus is saying, "Come on. Let's drop the pretenses. Let's get real here. I want to be your friend. I want to have fellowship with you. I want to spend time with you." He's saying, "I want to hang out with you. We'll order dessert and some coffee. I've got all the time in the world, and I'm interested in everything you have to say. I want fellowship, friendship, and intimacy with you."

That's intimacy. That is "God with us."

The very thought of this should touch us deeply. Just to think that God — the Almighty Creator of the universe — would be vitally interested in someone like you or me! To think that He actually wants to be a part of all we say and do! How could it be true? And yet, it is true. One of the songs I like to sing at this time of year is the old Christmas hymn "O Come, O Come, Emmanuel":

O come, O come, Emmanuel
And ransom captive Israel

That mourns in lonely exile here
Until the Son of God appear
Rejoice! Rejoice! Emmanuel
Shall come to thee, O Israel

O come, thou Wisdom from on high
And order all things far and nigh
To us the path of knowledge show
And teach us in her ways to go
Rejoice! Rejoice! Emmanuel
Shall come to thee, O Israel

We sing that. But do we want that? Do we? *Do we want Immanuel to come? Do we really want Him to be a part of our lives — not just Christmas, but all year long?* Christmas is coming, and . . . Christmas is almost over. The presents will be opened, and all that pretty paper will be in the trash can at the curb, along with the tree. You will soon be tired of those new toys and gadgets, and you'll move on to other things.

But if you have Immanuel, what does it matter?

Christmas comes and goes, but Immanuel stays forever.

NOTES

Introduction: The Color of Christmas
1. 2 Corinthians 9:15 (MSG).

Chapter 1: Before Bethlehem
1. C. S. Lewis, *The Voyage of the Dawn Treader* (New York: HarperCollins, 2000), 241.

Chapter 2: What's in a Name?
1. "Americans 'Need' Their Gadgets," *Wired*, December 21, 2005, http://www.wired.com/science/discoveries/news/2005/12/69896.
2. Max Lucado, *God Came Near* (Nashville: Thomas Nelson, 2008), 7.

Chapter 4: A Twisted Family Tree
1. Susan Brink, "Suicide: Holidays' Darkest Myth," *Los Angeles Times*, December 17, 2007, http://articles.latimes.com/2007/dec/17/health/he-xmasdepress17.
2. Ephesians 2:12, NIV.

Chapter 5: Don't Miss Christmas
1. Psalm 10:4, NIV.
2. Mark 7:6-7, NIV.

Chapter 6: Don't Lose Jesus
1. Psalm 46:10.

Chapter 9: The Promise of Christmas
1. C. S. Lewis, *Made for Heaven: And Why on Earth It Matters* (New York: HarperCollins Publishers, 2005), 19–20.
2. There are many passages, including 1 Thessalonians 4:17 and Hebrews 12:22-23.

Other Books by Greg Laurie

As I See It
Better Than Happiness
Daily Hope for Hurting Hearts
Dealing with Giants
Deepening Your Faith
Discipleship
Essentials
For Every Season, volumes 1, 2, and 3
God's Design for Christian Dating
The Great Compromise
The Greatest Stories Ever Told, volumes 1, 2, and 3
His Christmas Presence
Hope
Hope for America
Hope for Hurting Hearts
How to Know God
I'm Going on a Diet Tomorrow
Living Out Your Faith
Making God Known
Married. Happily.
Run to Win
Secrets to Spiritual Success
Signs of the Times
Start! To Follow
Strengthening Your Faith
Ten Things You Should Know About God and Life
Upside Down Living
What Every Christian Needs to Know
Why, God?
Worldview

Visit: www.AllenDavidBooks.com